UNSTOPPABLE!

God's Grand Purpose Through the Life of John and Betty Banker

Kathy Banker Taber

A true story that displays what Job learned long ago

Then Job replied to the Lord:
"I know that you can do all things;
no purpose of yours can be thwarted."
Job 42:1-2

© 2021 by Kathy Banker Taber

ISBN 978-1-716-43777-9

Published by Kathy Banker Taber
Dallas, Texas

Available for purchase at Lulu.com

Cover design by Karen K. Tawa
Cover art by Thomas J. Banker
Photos inherited from John and Betty Banker's personal collection

Printed in the United States of America

All rights reserved. No part of this publication may be reproduced, stored in a retrieval system, or transmitted in any form or by any means—for example, electronic, photocopy, recording—without the prior written permission of the publisher. The only exception is brief quotations in printed reviews.

Unless otherwise indicated, Scripture is taken from the Holy Bible, New International Version®, NIV® Copyright 1973, 1978, 1984, 2011 by Biblica, Inc.™ Used by Permission. All rights reserved worldwide.

To the memory of my loving parents,
John and Betty Banker,
who by their lives taught me to trust in the
sovereignty of God
and His good purpose in all things
no matter what.

*And we know that in all things God
works for the good of those who love him,
who have been called according to his purpose.*
Romans 8:28

*For we are God's handiwork, created in
Christ Jesus to do good works,
which God prepared in advance for us to do.*
Ephesians 2:10

*You did not choose me, but I chose you
and appointed you so that you might
go and bear fruit—fruit that will last.*
John 15:16

UNSTOPPABLE!

Acknowledgements

Before you read a word, I want to express my appreciation to all those who helped bring this book about, pushing me forward to do better work even when I was ready to be done, and to God who gave me the strength and ability to keep on keeping on.

I want to thank Vurnell Cobbey and Carolyn Miller who provided editorial input with the eyes of those who had personally experienced many of the events in this book.

I want to thank my husband Mark for his help in editing, scanning and inserting the photos, doing all the layout and formatting, and helping me publish this book. His brother, Wes Taber, gave me many excellent discourse level suggestions to make it more vivid and flow better. Many thanks as well to Dee Parker for her careful editing of all the jots-and-tittles.

The artwork on the cover was beautifully done by my brother Tom Banker. Thank you, Tom, for capturing one of our childhood memories so well. I also want to thank my daughter Karen Tawa for designing the cover.

Thank you, Mom and Dad; your lives inspired this book, and your careful recording and preserving so many written details has made this project possible.

And finally, all praise be to God, whose unstoppable plan brought about these events and encouraged me to record them here. May He be greatly praised because of His marvelous deeds!

UNSTOPPABLE

Preface

Douglas Welsh ends his book, The History of the Vietnam War (Simon & Schuster, 1985), with these words:

> The Vietnam War was a violent era in American history on which much will eventually be written. A final understanding will only be reached when attempts to fix the blame against the Government, the military, the people and the media can be set aside.
>
> Perhaps understanding will only come when all those who have lived through the experience are dead and the facts can be assessed more objectively. It will be at least a generation before "Vietnam" will mean anything but a war of agony, frustration, and humiliation.

This book provides another perspective on that era in history. It includes "agony, frustration, and humiliation" yet not purposelessness, hopelessness or futility. This book is an account of how God, in every situation, is always working out His master plan, taking what was meant for evil and turning it into good.

My prayer is that this book will be a means of bringing healing and hope, increasing faith and faithfulness, and pulling back the curtain that often blocks our view so that we can better see the glory of God magnified through His unstoppable purpose.

The primary source for this book is the many letters written by John and Betty Banker back home to family every week from 1958 until 2015. Quotations from these letters have been formatted to be easily identifiable. Some of the other details were filled in from conversations with Betty and taken from many of her other written materials in the form of diary or the form of presentations that she or John made for various audiences over the years. Some of John's early history came from a written account by his brother James (Jim) Banker.

Since, as one of John and Betty's children, I (Kathy) am included in these letters and their story, I have chosen to refer to myself using the third person. This includes when I share my own experiences based on personal memory. In this way I hope to avoid the subtle temptation as the author to shift the focus toward me. The only exception is the Epilogue at the end where I share from my heart in the first person.

Most of the story of Tet 1968 was taken from Betty's letters that she wrote home to family immediately following those harrowing events. A few details were filled in from others who were there at that time. This includes excerpts from the book *Captured!* by Carolyn Miller (1977) along with personal communication with her, as well as a write-up by Doris Blood, and a formal write-up in the group's missionary letter at that time. Information was also gathered from video clips of interviews with Ken and Marilyn Gregerson.

Some other background information regarding Tet 68, both in Kontum and other areas of the country as well as other background stories, come from the book *By Life or By Death* by James C. Hefley (1969). This includes some numbers, dates and direct quotes. In a few cases indirect quotes were made direct.

UNSTOPPABLE!

Whenever possible the author attempted to confirm secondary accounts by comparing them with those who had personally experienced them. Information was taken from written communication from Janie Voss in connection with the evacuation of orphans in 1975, and with Kermit Titrud in connection with refugees from Vietnam after 1975. A letter from Freddy Boswell, Executive Director for SIL, and from the Bahnar people following John Banker's death are also included. Excerpts are also included from several regular missionary newsletters. Several other books referred to include: *The Joy of a Loving Jonathan* and *Sadie Busse Sieker,* which are listed in the sources at the end of the book.

The majority of the photographs come from John and Betty Banker's personal collection and are included with permission. A few photos are from the author's own collection.

The personal names of people as well as names of villages from the minority people groups in Viet Nam have been changed to protect their privacy. All other names and locations are real and have not been changed.

UNSTOPPABLE!

John's Early Years (1934-56)

On March 9, 1934 John was born in Plattsburgh New York, the first child of Marion K. (Vaughan) and John James Banker. Within the next four years a sister and two brothers joined their family. Their parents owned an apple orchard and truck garden, so very early in life John learned to work hard and be responsible, habits that influenced his whole life and ministry.

When John was only four, the tanks of George Patton's Tank Corps rumbled their way up to the Plattsburgh area and practiced their maneuvers in the Banker fields. A few years later, when John was in second grade, World War II began.

John was a young boy when he first started helping out on the Banker farm and apple orchard. His father gave him the task of riding their horse, Rex, and guiding the horse down the vegetable rows while he held the handle of the cultivator, making sure he was taking out the weeds and not the vegetables. John also worked with Rex and the dump rake to rake hay. John had to be careful to rake at the right time so that the row would be straight. This was hard work for a young boy. One day a sudden storm rolled in. Lightning flashed and thunder crashed! Startled, Rex galloped for his barn a half mile away. He dragged the rake down the road all the way.

UNSTOPPABLE!

In early spring when John was eight years old, he along with some of his siblings and his cousin Bob were playing in the hay barn. John's father, also named John, climbed onto a tractor parked next to the barn. When he turned the ignition, gas trickled out of the engine. The engine sparked, loose hay ignited, and a fire spread like wind. John's father shouted to the children, "Quick! Bob, help me get the cattle out of the barn! The rest of you, climb out through the broken board in the wall!"

One after another, the children quickly slid through the hole in the wall. Like a hungry ravenous beast, the fire enveloped the barn. John's father and Bob desperately struggled to save the cows as the barn blazed, burned, and crackled till it lay dead in ashes on the ground.

John and Bob rescued the terrified cattle in time. The children escaped, fleeing to safety. But no one knew what had happened to little John. After a concerned search, the family found him playing under a bed with his toy soldiers.

This was not John's only scary experience in that barn. One summer the men were drawing hay into the barn on great hay wagons. One wagon was already full of hay. A second one sat with just a small portion of the front end of the load, just inside the door.

John and his siblings liked to climb up on the square beams of the barn. John crawled onto the beam located just above the barn door. He made his way across that beam and held onto the boards of the front wall, steadying himself as he moved. As he slid his feet to the middle point of the door, suddenly he lost his footing and fell through the air. Seconds later he hit the front end of the load with a bang. There was nothing to stop him from falling all the way down onto the tongue of the wagon, right onto a bolt. He was shaken, but somehow, not badly hurt.

From the time John was young his special love for God was obvious to everyone, even his siblings. Jack, as he was known by his family, was very kind to his siblings and to everyone else. In the Banker family the things of God were treated as important, and each one of the family was expected to attend church. As well as the Sunday morning service, John's mother went to the Sunday evening service and prayer meeting on Wednesday night. John was the only one who accompanied her to these other services. He actually seemed to enjoy church more than most children and he was serious about living his faith.

John always treated the Word of God with great honor. In the Banker house a Bible was placed on a prominent table in the dining room and from time to time a magazine or something else would be carelessly placed on top of it. John would remove the magazine as soon as he saw it. Sometimes his siblings would tease him about this, but John never got angry.

[In later years his brother would say, "This was typical of John's manner with everyone, polite and respectful even when a person might not deserve it."]

As the oldest of the four Banker children, John was serious about keeping an eye on the safety and well-being of

UNSTOPPABLE!

the other children. Around the Banker farm, there lived some twenty children of various ages who often played and had adventures together. Sometimes they worked in the garden for their dad. Other times they looked for adventure elsewhere on their large property.

In the winter the kids went skiing below the orchard, on a hill with the perfect incline. One day some ten children decided to ski there. To make it more interesting they built their own ski jump about five feet high. One after another, the children all took turns flying over the jump. It was great fun until one of the girls, Florence, sailed off the jump, fell to the ground, and broke a limb. Sixteen-year-old John quickly instructed the rest of the children to strap together their skis to make a stretcher. Fourteen-year-old Florence was not light but, working together, the children carried her home so she could be taken to the hospital.

Another time, the children sauntered through the orchard then ducked into the woods to play games in the snow, coming at last to the frozen brook. Taking turns, they ran and slid back-and-forth across the cold, hard surface. Suddenly, John's younger brother, Jim, broke through the ice. In an instant he was totally immersed in the freezing water. Quickly John grabbed him out of the water, pulled him onto his back and carried him the one-half mile to the barn near the road. There, their parents picked Jim up and brought him home.

John and his siblings attended grade school in the nearby town at the Laboratory School of Plattsburgh Teachers

UNSTOPPABLE!

College. Although still in grade school, they took the bus with the high school children. One day one of the four Banker siblings lost a dime, which they needed to buy food while at school. They all searched and searched but could not find it.

Once again, John had a solution. He said, "I shall throw my dime down and watch where it goes, and the other dime will be there."

He flipped his dime in the air, and it landed on top of the lost dime! The siblings continued on to school, amazed at their older brother's wisdom.

The younger Banker siblings looked up to big brother John for his performance in school. He always received very high grades from his teachers. This laid the groundwork for his latter achievements in linguistics.

When John was 14, special services were held at his church. John went forward and asked God to forgive his sins and Jesus Christ to be his Savior. As John grew in his faith, he prayed that Jesus Christ would become pre-eminent in his life, that he would be more like Jesus and win others for Him; John chose to follow Jesus with his whole heart and life.

For most of John's young life he had thought that serving God was something a person did because God gave them a special calling. But John began to realize that people were to go tell others about Jesus because God already commands us in His Word to do so.

John originally thought he would become a pastor, but while a student at Houghton College, John felt God calling him to be a Bible translator. As a young man, God gave him Matthew 6:33 as the theme verse of his life. "But seek first his kingdom and his righteousness, and all these things will be given to you as well."

Between his junior and senior year of college John sandwiched a year of coursework needed to be a Bible Translator. He was accepted by Wycliffe Bible Translators in August 1956, and after graduation he set off for Jungle Camp training in Mexico. He looked to God to show him in which country and language group God wanted him to serve, so that they too could have God's Word in their own mother tongue, the language that speaks to their hearts.

Viet Nam

Missionaries had labored among the Vietnamese for many years. But there were not yet many who spoke the

UNSTOPPABLE!

languages of the Montagnard peoples[1] to do much ministry among them. Vietnamese preachers had zealously preached in isolated Montagnard villages. On occasion, when people understood the messages in the national language, some would believe.

---

[1] The Montagnard are the minority people groups who live in the central highlands of southern Viet Nam and are ethnically distinct from the Vietnamese people.

UNSTOPPABLE!

Two Montagnard people groups, the Koho and their Roglai neighbors were enemies, constantly at war with each other. A Koho couple wanted to stop this continual enmity. They bravely headed into Roglai territory where they persuaded a Roglai family to drink a blood covenant together with them. Both of these people groups had matrilineal social systems and so it was that two women, one Roglai and one Koho, drank each other's blood, making a peace pact between these two warring people groups.

Many years later the granddaughter of the Koho covenant maker came to believe in Jesus through Herbert Jackson. She desired to share this Good News with the Roglai people. Perhaps the blood covenant, which the two parties had made so many years before, might be a way to introduce the Good News to them.

[Photo: Daughter of the woman who made a blood covenant]

She made her way to the home of the grandson of the Roglai covenant maker, a well-known sorcerer. She asked if he remembered the past covenant between their two families, making peace between their two ethnic groups. He did indeed remember. Upon hearing this, she invited him to some evangelistic meetings in the Koho village. He attended the meetings and gave his heart to Christ.

UNSTOPPABLE!

From that time on when people came asking him to practice sorcery on their behalf, he encouraged them to believe in Jesus instead. As a result, forty Roglai people believed in Christ. In 1954, Herbert Jackson visited a Roglai village for the first time to share the Gospel. To his surprise, he discovered a group of believers worshipping God and witnessing to others.

Dick Pittman came to Viet Nam in 1956. He met with people from the government and other leaders, telling them of his vision and the mission of his organization to translate the Bible into the mother tongue of people from every language and people group. He wanted them to have God's Word in the language that spoke to their hearts. He also wanted to help produce dictionaries, grammars and literacy primers for educators and leaders in the church.

The President of Viet Nam accepted Dick's offer after reading a very positive letter from the President of the Philippines. The letter extolled the excellent linguistic, literacy, and translation work which Dick Pittman's organization had already done in the Philippines.

But these weren't easy days to be working in Viet Nam. By 1958 the anti-government guerillas had been causing unrest in the country. By 1959, soldiers who had fought against the French and moved north after the Geneva Peace settlement, came south again. They crossed the Demilitarized Zone (DMZ) and traveled through Laos. They dug up buried weapons and took on a new name—the Viet Cong.

UNSTOPPABLE!

A New Life Far from Home (1958)

John finished college and received training in linguistics, translation and jungle living. As part of John's training, he was assigned to partner with another single man translating the Bible for a language in Mexico. His job was to do the cooking so the other man would be free to focus on Bible Translation. This was a new experience for John who had never cooked before in his life.

In January of 1958, supported by the Turnpike Wesleyan Church in Plattsburgh, NY, John boarded a ship bound for the Philippines. He felt God was calling him to go to Viet Nam, however, his first stop was the Philippines, where he waited for his entry visa to Viet Nam.

While waiting, John joined another single man who was translating the Bible for a language community in the Philippines. Toward the end of that year, John received his visa and clearance to go to Viet Nam. He again boarded a ship and left Manila harbor on December 15, 1958, barely missing Betty Mundy who arrived five days later by ship.

Upon reaching Saigon, John joined a number of young missionaries hoping to do Bible translation in Viet Nam. On January 18, 1959, soon after his arrival, John wrote home to his parents:

UNSTOPPABLE!

> We have been here a month already. We are just getting under way in full-time language learning. We are now having classes in the morning and afternoon and three nights a week. We study about three hours in the morning, two hours in the afternoon, and two hours two days a week at night, and one hour the other nights.
>
> In the spare time I am helping out with the bookkeeping. I am really enjoying learning Vietnamese. I don't know much yet. In our classes we have a Vietnamese informant who goes over the lesson. We are supposed to speak it after him. He tells when we say things wrong. It takes a lot of mimicry. Then after an hour of this we listen to the lesson on a tape recorder. This is all done at our house. At night we go to a school and have class. The maids who do our cooking and washing and cleaning, really try to help us learn.
>
> Two more families arrived this week. Now we have children. The Haupers are living in the older house where we are living. Ralph Haupers was the fellow I came over with on the ship from the States. They have two children, one boy a little over two years old and a girl about nine or ten months. It is nice to have them here.

John wrote home every week to his family, whom he wouldn't see for six years. He shared the many things he was learning and doing, keeping his letters full of faith and thankfulness, despite difficult circumstances. In June, after being in Viet Nam for about six months, John wrote home:

> The Lord opened up many opportunities last week to witness for Him. One Chinese friend of mine is especially interested in knowing how his sins can be forgiven. He asked, "How can I become a good man?" I have tried to

explain the Gospel to him but he does not yet understand. So, pray that he might understand and believe. I also had opportunities to witness to some Vietnamese boys who are my friends.

Meanwhile, Betty Mundy had traveled by ship from Seattle in December 1958. Bad weather and high seas rocked the boat. Finally, the ship arrived in Tokyo, where Betty and others made their way to Kobe and again boarded a ship and headed to the Philippines.

Betty's Beginnings (1934-58)

Betty, who was born Elizabeth Frances Mundy on October 11, 1934, had grown up on a farm in rural Alberta, Canada. She was one of 11 children.

Betty is second from the left in the back

UNSTOPPABLE!

It was a busy household and Betty was the oldest girl, which came with a lot of responsibility. Her energetic younger siblings included two sets of twins. When she was five years old, her parents gave her a doll dressed as a nurse. From that day on a desire was lit in Betty's heart to be a nurse.

Betty's parents had never heard the message of God's saving grace; neither had Betty's Aunt Grace who lived in Chicago. One day she listened to a radio program from Moody Bible Institute where she heard the Good News about Jesus. Moved by His gracious gift of salvation, Grace accepted Jesus as her Savior. In time her husband and family also believed in Jesus. They prayed for many years that their relatives in Alberta, Canada would also come to know Him.

Following the great desire of their hearts that their relatives would also experience the joy of knowing Jesus, Betty's Aunt Grace and her family came to Alberta. Betty saw her parents sitting together in her aunt's car for long periods of time talking earnestly. When Betty was 12 years old, her parents placed their trust in the Lord Jesus Christ for forgiveness of their sins.

A year later in 1947, while attending Vacation Bible School, Betty understood the Gospel for the first time. She, too, trusted Jesus as her Savior and surrendered her life to following Him as her Lord.

Betty and her family lived far from any church that preached the Gospel. They did not own a car—only a horse and cart—so the church at Etzikom and Orian sent some young people to the Mundy home each week to lead them in a Bible Study. One week a missionary nurse, who worked in Africa, came with the young people. Because Betty wanted to be a nurse, she was very interested to hear what this visitor had to say. That night she heard God speaking to her through the words of the nurse from Africa. She knew in the depths of her heart that God wanted her to be a missionary, too.

But during Betty's high school years, she focused on reaching her dream of being a nurse. Biology was not taught in her high school, so she found a way to study this essential course by correspondence. Yet as she kept pushing toward her own dream, all the while God kept reminding her of the commitment she had made to serve Him as a missionary. She finally admitted to the Lord that she was being disobedient in wanting to follow her plan, not His.

After graduating from high school, Betty went to Prairie Bible Institute (PBI) in 1952. Each year she and the other students were required to work ten and a half hours per week to help pay for their room and board. In Betty's second year she was assigned to look after the many missionaries who came to speak in classes and chapels.

UNSTOPPABLE!

One day a couple serving with Wycliffe Bible Translators visited PBI. As Betty interacted with them, God spoke to her heart that His plan for her was to be involved in translating God's Word for a Bibleless people group.

All PBI students were required to take a Missions course in their junior year. Betty had never even heard of Viet Nam before. But as she studied about the missionary work among the indigenous people groups in the highlands of South Viet Nam, the Lord confirmed in her heart His call to her life's work. God wanted her to translate the Bible into one of those languages so that they too could understand His Word.

With Bible school finished, Betty went on to receive specialized training in linguistics and Bible translation. She learned to "rough it" outdoors through Jungle Camp training in Mexico. In addition to learning to survive without modern conveniences, Betty taught the children of a Mission Aviation Fellowship (MAF) pilot and helped with the Bible translation project among the Otomi people in Mexico.

One day Betty received a message that a man in Arizona designated money to be given to a single woman assigned to do Bible Translation in Viet Nam. At that time, Betty was the only single woman that fit that description. This specific gift of money from someone she did not know and who did not know anything about God's call on her life was a great encouragement.

God's message was clear, "Betty, you are going in the right direction; this is exactly how I want you to serve me and I will provide for all your needs."

UNSTOPPABLE!

Betty was learning through these years that finding God's call and purpose for her life was dependent on her taking one small step of obedience at a time. Each time as she said to God, "Not my will, but yours," and obeyed Him, He showed her the next step.

And as she learned to obey, the Lord confirmed to her heart that she was going in the right direction. Betty never did meet the man from Arizona who continued to support her until he went to be with the Lord several years later. But his gift of money would help her remain strong and confident numerous times in the years to follow. Many times during the war Betty and those she loved would be in grave danger. Yet she would not dwell in fear because she was following God's leading every step of the way.

In late 1958, Betty set sail by freighter for the Philippines, supported by Meeting Creek Church and the church of Etzikom and Orion in Alberta, Canada. She left from the West Coast of the U.S., accompanied by Alice Tegenfeld (Marriott). They passed through Japan on their way, arriving in Manila on Dec. 20th.

While awaiting her visa for Viet Nam, Betty again spent her time teaching missionary children. Two months later she was on a passenger ship headed for Viet Nam. After three days at sea, her ship docked in the port of Saigon in February 1959.

UNSTOPPABLE!

Surprised by Love (1959)

Each time a ship arrived bringing missionaries to serve in Viet Nam, the whole Bible translation bunch headed to the docks to meet the newcomers. Each young single man, John Banker among them, wondered if a pretty young woman arriving might someday be his wife. One young man even brought a wedding ring from his home country for this very purpose.

Also aboard Betty's ship were two other young single women, Jean Donaldson and Pat Bonnell. Upon arrival, the young ladies were taken to the rented house in which many of their colleagues were already living. Every room was full, so Betty, Pat and Jean slept in the hallway upstairs, with sheets hanging around them as "walls" for privacy.

Betty's early days in Viet Nam were not easy. She soon came down with dengue fever, interrupting her language learning. When she recovered from dengue, language learning was again slowed when she took on the job of house manager for the missionary home in which she and her colleagues were living. Each had different responsibilities in caring for all the practical running of the group house.

Betty worked during the day managing a full house, and at night she went to language school. She couldn't help but notice that John Banker was the star language learner in the group. One day the whole group chartered a bus to go to the beach for a picnic lunch. Betty was sitting on the beach when John came and sat beside her. They joined the volleyball game and John smashed the volleyball in her face a couple times.

On the way back, John didn't have a seat. Betty invited him to have a seat by her, but he wouldn't do it.

To spur matchmaking, the Haupers were playing cupid with all the single men: John Banker, David Blood, and John Miller. One day the Haupers asked Betty to come babysit. When they returned, they asked John to walk Betty home. That night John asked Betty out on their first date.

After that, every night they went for quiet walks in the peaceful park nearby and sat on the benches surrounded by greenery in the moonlight. One night, they got locked out of the group house and had to scramble up over the fence to get in.

Saigon was relatively safe at this time, but John and Betty heard stories about the Viet Cong (VC) coming into the villages to demand rice. The VC also killed educated people and school teachers. John and Betty began to see army tanks rolling and rumbling down the streets. The three years that they lived in Saigon (1959-61), the winds of war were brewing but had not yet begun to blow in earnest.

In August 1959, eight months after his arrival in Viet Nam, John wrote home to his parents:

> This last week we had our linguistic workshop. A paper I had written in February on Subanen is going to be published in a volume of Philippine Summer Institute of Linguistic papers for our 25th Anniversary year.
>
> Today I am very lonesome because Betty has gone to Dalat for a few days. I didn't tell you her last name before.

UNSTOPPABLE!

It's Mundy, but it won't be for long. In a few months her name will be Betty Banker, okay? She said it was okay. It's not public here yet. You and her folks are the first ones to know. We are going to try to keep it a secret for another month.

I'm sure you will like Betty although it will be another four years probably before you get to meet her. She is really a good cook, knows how to sew and all that, smart, too. She is short; 5 feet, 2 inches. Is she ever fast—especially when she's working around the house. She is always doing something for someone else. Does she ever have a cute smile.

Forgive me for bragging about her but I thought you might want to know a little about the new daughter you are getting, Mom and Dad, and about your new sister, Alice and Jim. I am very happy because I believe that she is God's choice for me.

With a wedding around the corner, Betty's father, Tom Mundy, wrote a letter to the Banker family of Plattsburgh, NY, saying:

You say that we must be a very religious family. I expect that you would probably be very surprised if you should visit with us. We are just everyday ordinary people who have accepted the Lord Jesus Christ, not only as Savior, but also as Lord. We have no occasion to depend upon our observances and works for our salvation so are free to serve Him because of our love for Him.

You will find that Betty is certainly not a self-righteous person, but that she is an entirely normal fun-loving girl. We are very positive that Jack [John] must be a very fine young man for Betty to have fallen in love with him, and we have certainly accepted him as one of us. A young man from British Columbia who we are pleased to call a very good friend, wrote to us from Brazil, where he is a missionary, to tell us that he had been in Jungle Camp with Jack [John]. And knowing that we had never met Jack, he wanted to assure us that Jack was as fine a chap as he had ever met. Mr. Dick Pittman also wrote to us from Saigon to tell us the same thing.

I teach the adult class in our church and have for ten or twelve years, and we are quite willing that the Lord should take as many of our family as He pleases into full time service for Him. Preferably to the foreign field where, we feel, that the need is the greatest.

On Friday, November 27th, 1959, John and Betty were wed. The pews of the church were decorated with white fans and satin bows with daisies. A motto in black and gold letters read, "One in Christ."

In fact, John and Betty had already been married legally since Monday afternoon earlier in the week, when the mayor had performed the country's required civil ceremony in a "courtroom." There was no doubt that God had brought them together and had a special plan for their lives.

UNSTOPPABLE!

God's Guiding Hand (1959-60)

In early November, a couple weeks before the wedding, John and colleague, Milton (Milt) Barker, had gone on a five-day trip. The Land Rover took them over 2,000 kilometers (1,200 miles) on both good and bad roads. John wrote in a letter home to his parents:

> It was a long, weary drive, but about the most beautiful drive I've ever had. In places we were right beside the ocean just barely above it and sometimes away up on the side of a mountain almost directly above the ocean.
>
> We saw a lot of tribal people along the roads. You can tell tribal people because they are decked in different type of clothing. Other characteristics are that usually they carry pack baskets on their backs and that they seemed to be scared of cars. Some of their ears have big earrings. The men sometimes wear loincloths.

Around noon they came to the remains of a bridge. In place of the washed-out bridge, the local people had taken four handmade row boats and laid planks across the top. In this way they constructed a makeshift ferry with which to take vehicles across the river. John and Milt took their car over the river on the "ferry" and continued on their way.

UNSTOPPABLE!

Later in the afternoon, once again they found their route blocked, this time by a large fallen tree. With no way to navigate their vehicle around the blockage they backed up and took another route which brought them through the town of Pleiku.

In Pleiku lived Gail and Irene Fleming, members of the Christian & Missionary Alliance (C&MA) mission. They had recently begun their assignment to plant churches among the Bahnar people of Pleiku. When they heard that John and Betty were seeking God's will regarding which people group He would have them translate the Bible for, the Flemings invited John and Betty to come join their team. Their desire was that the Bahnar church would also have God's Word in their language.

It was no coincidence that a tree blocked the road that day. John and Betty saw God's hand in this whole trip and felt that He was indeed calling them to translate the Bible for the Bahnar people. John returned to Saigon where he and Betty were still serving their colleagues as house manager and bookkeeper, awaiting God's timing for when they could be free to begin the task of translating the Bible for the Bahnar people.

One day Betty climbed onto her bicycle and pedaled toward Cholon, the Chinese city next to Saigon. It was 1960 and Betty was pregnant with their first child. She arrived at a corner where seven roads met together in a roundabout sort of fashion. With no discernible rules about right-of-way, Betty pedaled forward into the intersection.

UNSTOPPABLE!

Suddenly, a taxi bore down on her at high speed. There was no time to move. In an instant the car and bike inexplicably changed positions—from perpendicular to parallel. Betty was suddenly even with the driver's window, though she didn't know how. She saw the shocked look of disbelief on the face of the driver as he zoomed by without hitting her. A bit shaken, Betty thanked God for His unseen, yet ever-present, protection.

In January 1960 John wrote home telling the family that the Lord was leading them to the Bahnar people; one of the more influential and better-known minority people groups of Viet Nam. However, John was still filling in as the group bookkeeper in their Saigon office. It would still be some time before they could move to the central highlands and start learning the Bahnar language.

One night they went to a Vietnamese wedding reception. To John's great joy, they met someone who was able to introduce them to a Bahnar man studying in Saigon. John praised the Lord for this opportunity to begin learning the Bahnar language, even though they were still so far from Bahnar territory.

February 14, 1960 John wrote home to his family:

Betty is really a wonderful wife. The Lord knew what I needed. We had a good time today. After American church we went out to the floating restaurant which is on a boat in the river. But since the tide was out it wasn't floating. Then we walked around Saigon some and went

UNSTOPPABLE!

to the zoo. It was good to get out and we really enjoyed ourselves. The zoo is outside and not inside a building at all. Saigon has a lot of trees that make it shady.

We certainly appreciate your prayers for the pregnancy. The Lord has been helping us in many ways. How wonderful He has been and how we praise Him for all He has done. Betty and I are certainly very happy. I know that you will think of her as your own daughter.

God's Perfect Timing (1960)

In early 1960, not too long after John and Betty were married, fellow colleagues, Milton and Muriel Barker, offered to temporarily fill in to do the Bankers' group service jobs. With Barkers taking over the bookkeeping and managing the group house John and Betty were able to make a trip to Pleiku to learn more of the Bahnar language and culture in preparation to do Bible translation.

When they arrived in the town of Pleiku, the District Chief gave the Bankers permission to stay in the Bahnar village of Kreilawna. To keep an eye on their safety, two Vietnamese soldiers would live with John and Betty in the communal "guest" house.

UNSTOPPABLE!

The Bankers did not know that the communal house was the dormitory for boys who had reached puberty, along with bachelors and men who were visiting the village. They also weren't aware that normally women were forbidden in the communal house.

One night they got up to go relieve themselves outside. They slipped past the blanket that had been hung for their privacy and found, to their surprise, the floor full of sleeping men and boys!

The Bankers received permission to stay in the village twice for two weeks at a time. Each time, for their safety, they were guarded by Vietnamese soldiers.

In September, John and Betty took another trip together to Pleiku hoping to spend another couple of weeks in Kreilawna. Upon arrival, they asked the District Chief, who happened to be Bahnar, for permission to go to the village. But this time permission was denied because it was too dangerous for foreigners to live away from the protection of the cities. Instead, he put them up in a little house on the District Center compound and sent his younger brother Om to teach them Bahnar. This was the beginning of a lifelong friendship with Om and his extended family.

UNSTOPPABLE!

Back in Saigon once again, on Oct 30, 1960 John wrote to his parents:

> We are now living in one of the new rooms on the balcony of the [group] house. In the day it is quite hot in the room because there is no fan although the room is quite open.

Because new families were arriving to serve in Viet Nam and the group had not yet been able to find a new house to rent, the group continued to add on new makeshift rooms. In these sleeping conditions, the hot sticky tropical nights were frequently oppressive.

[Many of these families were living in the group house together]

At this time, it was still considered safe in the city, but occasionally there was unrest. On November 13, 1960, John again wrote to his parents from Saigon:

> We are safe and sound here and praise the Lord for it. We went to church this morning. Everything is peaceful now and things are getting back to normal. Our hearts are thankful to the Lord for His protection during this time. I

hope that you did not worry too much. A telegram was sent to our headquarters in Santa Ana from where you were supposed to have received a telegram saying that we were all safe.

There had been an attack on the President's palace which was located just on the other side of the park near the group house where they were living. John and Betty's room was on the veranda with just a woven thatched wall around them and a covering made from old parachutes overhead. During the attack they could see the tracers flying over their heads as they lay in bed. Searching for a safer spot, they slipped inside the main part of the house. In the morning a tracer bullet landed with a bang in a washing machine located in the patio between the house and the kitchen.

Betty later would say, "This was the story of life in Viet Nam—calm followed by chaos repeated over and over again."

On December 14, 1960, John wrote to his parents:

I guess you got our telegram about Tommy's birth yesterday. He weighed 6 pounds 6 ounces, and is 20½ inches long. Everybody says he looks like a Banker. When I first saw him, I thought he looked a little like Jim. Betty said she thought he looked like you, Mom, and then tonight I thought he looked a lot like Daddy. The last 12 hours were quite rough. He was born face up so it made it quite a bit harder. I got to see most of the delivery.

UNSTOPPABLE!

Tonight I held him for the first time. What a wonderful thing it is to have a son of your own. How we praise the Lord for this gift from Him.

He is the first Banker [by blood] that I have seen in a long time. I'm glad that I have such a good wife. Tommy is going to have a wonderful mother.

Winds of War (1961-62)

The first U.S. troops arrived in Viet Nam in 1961. Three days before Christmas the first U.S. soldier was killed, just a few weeks after the troops arrived. The Viet Cong guerrilla attacks intensified as did the presence of U.S. troops called "advisors."

In the larger cities, life seemed to go on as normal. However, in rural areas it was a bit different. Missionaries had to be careful while going about their work and when they were traveling; they might be shot for being mistaken as American civilian advisers. This was very different from the situation during the French Indochina War, when the guerillas were favorable to Americans. Now it was getting dangerous for anyone with white skin, even missionaries.

Approximately a year after the District Chief in Pleiku had provided a place at the District Center compound for John and Betty to stay during their visit, they again came in contact with the chief's brother, Om. By this time others had taken over John and Betty's group service jobs in Saigon, freeing them to move to Pleiku for full-time study of the Bahnar language and culture.

UNSTOPPABLE!

Their first night in Pleiku, the Bankers stayed in the "long house" with Charlie and E.G. Long, C&MA missionaries to the Jarai people. [It was called this not because the Longs lived there, but because it was long.]

With Long's help, they found a duplex with one room on one side and two rooms on the other side; a little outhouse stood out back. The Bankers would live for several years in this little home located on the north end of Pleiku with open country beyond. In the distance was a Jarai village. They had very little furniture but did have a mattress and a warm quilt. John, Betty and baby Tommy all slept together and were able to keep warm.

Eventually their furniture arrived from Saigon. A large cupboard divided the one-room into a kitchen/dining area; the other half served as the living room/study/all-purpose room. They cooked on a two-burner kerosene stove and baked in a metal oven placed on top of these burners. Since both John and Betty had grown up on farms and loved open spaces, they loved to take baby Tommy for walks in the open field beyond their house.

Om came to work with John and Betty every day. He had a huge servant heart. In addition to teaching John and Betty the Bahnar language he also did whatever else he saw needed to be done. With no running water in the house, Om took buckets to the pump on the corner down the street and carried all the water needed by the family.

UNSTOPPABLE!

Om loved to take care of Tommy and Tommy loved Om. One of Tom's first words was, "d'Om." As Tommy (and eventually his siblings) always referred to him as "Uncle Om."

By 1962 the Viet Cong were infiltrating the area around Ban Me Thuot, Pleiku, Dalat, and Kontum. They would slip into the villages at night.

In the jungle near Ban Me Thuot, the C&MA leprosarium was located. It was not in a secure area, but as yet had not been touched. The C&MA missionaries helped hundreds of Montagnard people. Nowhere else in the highlands could this kind of medical treatment be obtained.

In 1960 the Bankers' colleagues, Hank and Vange Blood, began studying one of the other Montagnard languages. These people lived around a beautiful lake surrounded by mountains south of the city of Ban Me Thuot. Hank and Vange and their children lived in the back of a rented store.

After the Bloods spent two or three years studying the language, guerillas attacked the village one night. The family was aroused from sleep when shots rang out. Suddenly, they heard someone break into their store.

As they crouched behind a wall, the storefront became the command center from which the Viet Cong gave orders for their attack.

As the enemy overran the village, God brought to Hank's mind the story of Job, reminding Hank that Job was delivered when he prayed for his friends. So Hank and Vange prayed for hours for their friends in grave danger in the village.

UNSTOPPABLE!

The Viet Cong never discovered Hank and Vange whose two small children miraculously stayed quiet that whole time. By two in the morning the guerillas were gone and the lives of each of those Hank and Vange prayed for were spared.

Several months later the Bloods left their village to attend a linguistic conference in Saigon. They had planned to return on a Friday but ended up staying another day to shop. When they returned, they were told that the Viet Cong had come looking for them the night before.

The Bloods continued to study the language and began to translate some Bible stories as their first step in translation. Next, they began translating the Gospel of Mark with a young Christian named Talla. Eventually, they moved to Ban Me Thuot about 30 miles away which seemed to have better security.

Just north of Ban Me Thuot in the town of Pleiku, Betty Banker became pregnant with her second child. For her prenatal check-ups she went to Dr. Ardel Vietti, who served at the leprosarium near Ban Me Thuot. A check-up initially revealed everything to be fine. But on the first of April, John wrote home to his parents that the doctor had subsequently encouraged Betty to get her blood sugar levels checked again at the hospital in Saigon.

Further testing in Saigon revealed no problems. However, John and Betty wondered whether God was leading them to have the baby in Saigon, instead of at the leprosarium.

UNSTOPPABLE!

It was a timely decision. In the next couple of weeks, enemy soldiers overran the leprosarium in Ban Me Thuot and abducted Dr. Ardel Vieti, the doctor who was planning to deliver John and Betty's second child. They also captured several other missionaries serving there. None of them ever returned.[2]

Nevertheless, these events did not thwart God's purpose from being accomplished.

Getting Started on Translation (1962)

When John and Betty went to Saigon for Kathy's birth in late July 1962, Om, the brother of the District Chief in Pleiku went with them. While John was visiting Betty in the hospital, they would look out the window and there was Om holding Tommy in the yard.

Om was always there when needed. He became like a member of their family, very much loved and appreciated by all. Wherever John and Betty went, whether to conferences or workshops, Om accompanied them. They would always curtain off a corner of their room for his bedroom.

---

[2] A fuller story about the Bloods, Dr. Vieti, and others in Ban Me Thuot is in *By Life or By Death* (Hefley, 1969).

UNSTOPPABLE!

In John and Betty's orientation, the importance of cleanliness and sterilization had been emphasized in order to prevent serious illnesses. After Tommy was born, Betty was diligent and constantly worried about exposing Tommy to germs. This was not always easy, as people couldn't resist touching Tommy's curly blond hair, pinching his white cheeks, holding his hands and sharing food with him that they had already put in their mouths.

Keeping things clean became even more of an effort when Tommy began to crawl. Betty always tried to keep the floor clean before Tommy was let down to move about. One day she looked into his room and was greeted by his big smile. Beside him on the floor was half of a cockroach. The rest, Tommy had already swallowed.

Through events like this Betty felt God was showing her that Tommy was really His child. He was just loaning Tommy to her. She would care for Tommy the best she could but stop trying to do God's job. Entrusting her children to God's care was a habit that she would be learning repeatedly in the years to follow.

UNSTOPPABLE!

The Bankers' thin-layered cement floor developed pock-marked dirt potholes. Kathy, who crawled all over these floors, became very sick with an intestinal infection. She cried all night as John and Betty earnestly prayed, taking turns pacing back and forth across the floor holding their very ill child in their arms. Even the house helper cried out to God on her behalf.

The next day John and Betty took Kathy to Pat Smith, a doctor at the Catholic hospital. She treated Kathy, who quickly got better. Gravely, Doctor Smith informed them that without treatment they would surely have lost their little girl.

At this time around 75,000-85,000 Bahnar were living in the central highlands near Kontum, Pleiku and An Khe. In early 1962 there had been only two known Bahnar Christians, a man and his wife. Wokni had heard the gospel from the C&MA missionaries in the late 40s to early 50s. Together he and his wife strived many years to reach their own people with the Gospel, but saw no fruit. They left to do ministry among a different ethnic group, leaving no Bahnar believers in the area.

Three leprosy clinics were located in Pleiku and staffed by Alliance and Mennonite medical personnel. The Gale Flemings and the David Fraziers were the first Alliance missionaries planting churches among the Bahnar. Now they were joined by John and Betty who came to translate the Bible into the Bahnar language.

About once a week the Bankers translated one of the simpler Bible stories, and the C&MA missionaries used them right away in their ministry. Some very capable young men attended the Bible studies. As years went by, they were to become the backbone of the Church.

One Bahnar man, Kniah'a had the dreaded disease of leprosy. Compassionate C&MA missionaries brought him to the leprosarium in Ban Me Thuot. He was healed of leprosy and believed in Jesus.

After finishing Bible school, Kniah'a went home to his leper village and became a pastor. Eventually he was pastoring four congregations, even though people were often ambushed on the highway he traveled to these villages to preach.

Around this time, Wokni and his wife again returned to Bahnar territory. Even as the unrest of a coming war began to bubble and boil, a mighty work among the Bahnar was rising. By the end of 1962 about ten Bahnar had professed their faith in Jesus. The small Bahnar church continued to grow so that by 1963, the Alliance church planting missionaries had baptized over 100 Bahnar believers. However, there were many challenges to their faith. When someone in the villages became sick, accusations were thrown at these believers for making the spirits angry and causing trouble for others.

By May 1962 John and Betty had completed nine months of Bahnar language study and soon had 3,300 words in their Bahnar dictionary. [Previous beginnings at translation in the Bahnar language were known. Ten years earlier a Vietnamese had translated Mark along with Genesis, which was later retranslated by a Bahnar. The Catholics had produced a draft of Acts.]

Now John and Om continued the translation work and then used the scripture portions in Bible studies as soon as they finished translating them. They translated the story of Jesus stilling the storm from Mark chapter four and started a Bible study with their Bahnar teacher, Om, and their house helper, Itelli who showed great interest. Om said that he wished all of the people in his village would become Christians so they wouldn't drink so much. John and Betty prayed much for him and trusted that he, too, would soon believe in Jesus.

The Bankers also reached out to their Vietnamese neighbors in Pleiku. Several high school boys came a couple nights each week for English lessons, as well as a priest who was studying in seminary. John and Betty invited their Vietnamese friends to church, trusting that they, too, would search and find Jesus as their Savior.

While John worked on translation, Betty was developing Bahnar primers to train the people in literacy, so they could read the scriptures once translated. Om was a good artist and capably drew the illustrations. They produced about 180

UNSTOPPABLE!

pages of Bahnar stories, in which both animals and people took part and talked.

In October 1962 John wrote home:

> This has been an interesting week. On Tuesday I saw the Chief of Province and he said that we would be able to live in a tribal village. He said we would have to see the Chief of District about it first. We went to see him yesterday but he wasn't at home. The Chief of Province seemed to think that this tribal village would be good and safe.
>
> This morning we went to see the Chief of District and he said that we wouldn't be able to live in a tribal village, so I guess we will now see about living in a tribal village near Kontum or in Kontum itself. We ought to have better contact with the Bahnar there.

He also wrote:

> Did you ever see horses riding a bicycle? Tommy did. At least that is what he said yesterday as we were walking down the street. Actually, it was a couple of oxen pulling an oxcart. But it's hard to tell the difference between horses and cows when you're little, and doesn't an oxcart

have two wheels so isn't it a bicycle and what do you do to a bicycle but ride it?

A big four engine transport plane just landed at the new airstrip here. Tom and I went outside to see it as it passed by. There are a lot of planes landing here every day. Pleiku is a communications center for this area. It has a radar and several large transmitters so that from all over the area things can be radioed here and then retransmitted to more distant places.

The other day was Independence Day and among other things two small fighters were doing air stunts. I was invited to attend the ceremonies but didn't go. However, at night I attended the Chief of Province's reception. It was held outdoors and there was quite a crowd. I spent most of the time talking to some of my old friends—Mr. Ke who used to come to study English and I also talked to the Vietnamese doctor. Also, I met some new people including one of the American army officers.

Those at the US Army base were very good to the Bankers and others, inviting them for Thanksgiving dinner where they enjoyed a feast of good food not normally available to them.

Due to security issues, it was difficult to get permission to live in a Bahnar village near Pleiku. In September 1962 John and Om took a trip to the city of Kontum about 30 miles further north of Pleiku to see about staying in a village in that area.

They visited two Bahnar villages right on the edge of Kontum. The houses there were much bigger and better built than most Bahnar dwellings. Some were made of brick covered with plaster like many of the houses of the

UNSTOPPABLE!

Vietnamese. However, even these houses were high off the ground and held up by sturdy posts, unlike Vietnamese homes. [Most Montagnard houses were constructed with bamboo as in the photo.]

On November 30th the Bankers moved up to Kontum but, once again, due to security reasons they could not get permission to live in a village. Instead, they picked out a house in the city less than a quarter mile from two Bahnar villages, providing regular contact with the Bahnar people. At least five Bahnar villages, all Catholic, bordered Kontum with several others not far away.

Om accompanied the Bankers from Pleiku. He continued to be a faithful language teacher and translation helper for John. He also helped Betty make primers and language lessons to teach the Bahnar to read, as well as descriptions of the Bahnar grammar.

One day an American man who worked with the International Voluntary Service in connection with the U.S. government came to get copies of the Bahnar primers Betty and Om had produced. He wanted to start a reading class for the Bahnar men. His focus was agriculture and he hoped to produce a Bahnar agricultural handbook to help the people.

But first the Bahnar men would have to learn to read if they were to benefit from it.

The War Hits Closer to Home (1962-63)

For their first Christmas in Pleiku, the Bankers were invited to the U.S. Army compound for dinner. Toward the end of 1962 the war had been quickly escalating. The Viet Cong took over village after village leaving less and less secure government territory. Traveling the roads became increasingly unsafe.

By early 1963 Om had come to faith in Jesus and was attending church regularly. He also listened to a Christian broadcast in Vietnamese produced by the Far East Broadcasting Company in Manila. Singing and a message were followed by some English language instruction. Om's ability to speak English improved more quickly with the added benefit of listening to John and Betty and the children conversing in their home.

More missionaries were venturing to Viet Nam to translate the Bible for those who had none in their own languages. Among the new arrivals were Elwood Jacobsen and his wife Vurnell. After finishing university, Elwood wrote:

> Humility is making status irrelevant in the favor of more important considerations—serving people. Our service will never effectively communicate Jesus Christ if our status confuses the issue. Servants are non-status people. In the whole process of humbling one's self a man need never fear that he will suffer loss. In the economy of life,

he who loses his life finds it. For every experience of life, we must realize that we are in God's care.

Elwood had married Vurnell in 1961. His wedding vow to her had been: "I dedicate our lives to the honor of Jesus Christ our Lord who first loved us and gave Himself for us."[3]

A young Filipino man, Gaspar Makil, also came to translate the Bible for the Bibleless peoples of Viet Nam. He and his two cousins had been named after the three wisemen, Melchior, Gaspar and Balthazar. He had fought with Filipino guerrillas in WWII against the Japanese occupation of the Philippines. With the rest of his company Gaspar had secretly snuck desperately needed medicine, food and news to starving American prisoners held by the Japanese. One was a missionary whom Gasper and his fellow soldiers helped escape to freedom.

Despite the atrocities of war he had witnessed, Gasper held no grudge against the Japanese. After the war was over, a group of extremist students gathered to plan a surprise attack on a Japanese visitor to their country. Even though Gasper's cousin had been killed by the Japanese and his home burned, Gasper reasoned with the students, convincing them not to harm this Japanese man.

Gaspar received a partial scholarship to further his mechanical engineering studies in the U.S. To help cover the cost of the rest of his studies, a family member mortgaged his rice fields.

---

[3] This quote and the following quotes and facts in this section are taken from *By Life or By Death* (Hefley, 1969).

UNSTOPPABLE!

While in the U.S. Gaspar wrote:

> I do not pray for long life on this side of the grave. How you live that life is the thing that matters, not how long. That life is Christ's. I used to think of Christianity as a theory to be preached. Now I know that it is a life to be lived. The standard of that life is high but we can live it by the power of God working in us.

Not long before Gaspar left for Viet Nam, he told his pastor:

> I am ready to go. I believe it is God's will in my life, but I am afraid, somehow. Not for myself, but for my dear wife and our children. But men are dying over there without Christ; few have ever heard of Him. I must go. Pray for me.

Gaspar and his wife Josephine and family, and Elwood and Vurnell and their baby girl Kari arrived in Viet Nam just one month apart [Elwood and Kari in photo]. Little did they know how closely their lives would be connected.

The Makils felt the Lord calling them to work among the Southern Roglai people of Viet Nam. Gaspar was very excited when they received permission from the local officials to actually live in the village and begin to learn the language and culture of the people. Later he would write:

UNSTOPPABLE!

In Viet Nam there is much that wars against us each day, unfriendly forces from the outside, wasted time and energy on secondary matters, fears from within when we did not see much of the results of our labors. In my years as a Christian, the Lord has never let me know beforehand the next step I should take. But his guidance has always been sure as I have looked back and have seen my footsteps. And I believe that this is the way it should be because our Christian life is a life of faith. We put our foot forward in faith.

One day Elwood offered to drive Gaspar and Josephine Makil back to their home near Dalat [Gaspar and children in photo]. The road was declared to be safe by the military advisors posted along the highway. Other missionaries had been safely traveling that road at that time. So on March 4 1963, Elwood and his family accompanied the Makils on their journey.

Proceeding on their way, they encountered a roadblock. A dozen men wearing dark peasant pajama-like clothes signaled them off the road and began to question them. The sound of a helicopter and a South Vietnamese truck approaching spurred on a sudden round of shots. Elwood,

UNSTOPPABLE!

Gaspar, and one of Gaspar's twin daughters were hit and killed.

Hearing of the sorrowful loss of precious colleagues, Dr. Richard Pittman said:

> Those who killed them killed men who had come to Viet Nam to serve the underprivileged. The two knew how, by the grace of God, to love even their enemies. We are now blood brothers of the Vietnamese, because our blood has been shed with theirs for their people.

The deaths of Elwood and Gaspar on the Saigon-Dalat Highway occurred less than a year after the capture of the missionaries from the Ban Me Thuot leprosarium. Believers from the missionaries' home countries began to pray even more intensely for those serving in Viet Nam. Others begged them to come home.

Nancy Frieberger, who was translating the Bible for the Nung refugees from North Viet Nam, wrote:

Nancy Freiberger with Nung friend

> Do you really want us to come home? Do you really believe the Lord wants us to quit when the going gets rough? If you are more worried about our physical dangers than the souls that are being lost daily without ever hearing of Jesus Christ, you cannot pray with conviction and faith for the Lord to use us here, because your heart's cry is for us to be in the place of home safety. When we count the cost, do we not take into account there might be some physical loss—some distresses for the sake of Christ—some sharing in his sufferings? Or is it

just platform talk to make Christianity sound sacrificial and wonderful?

Throughout 1963, more than 2,000 assassinations and 7,000 kidnappings rocked South Viet Nam. Most of those killed were people of influence who refused to submit to the Viet Cong. Day or night, the VC could emerge from the jungle bringing terror and death.

On April 7, 1963, John wrote home to his parents:

> The Lord is blessing and protecting in all our work here. The widows of the two that were killed continue to be a real testimony to us and the others of the comfort the Lord has given.

Betty's faith was strengthened and her courage grew when she saw how Josephine and Vurnell continued to serve the Lord in Bible translation despite the tragic loss of their husbands.

By the end of 1963, 41 Bible translators sent by Wycliffe had arrived in Viet Nam. Bible translation had already begun in 14 languages. God was at work expressing His unfailing love and fulfilling His kingdom purpose to make His Word available to the minority peoples of Viet Nam despite—and even because of—growing conflict.

Moving Forward (1963-66)

In August 1963, John and Betty left for the city of Hue to attend a linguistic workshop. Along with three other translation teams and their language assistants, they spent

UNSTOPPABLE!

time writing up the grammars of the languages each was studying. John wrote home:

> I finally finished my paper on Bahnar clauses yesterday, and am very thankful for the Lord's help in getting it done. Now, when we go back to Kontum and get settled in we can continue on translation.
>
> We would appreciate your prayers that we might have a profitable workshop so that we will be better equipped for translating the Word of God. We would appreciate prayer for wisdom as we do trial translation.

After the workshop finished in November the Bankers returned to Kontum to translate the first edition of the Gospel of Mark. This book was selected first because it was the easiest book to translate and it clearly explains the Gospel story. When their completed draft was checked by a Bible translation consultant many things were found that needed to be fixed. John and Betty still had much to learn about the translation process.

At this time more terrorist attacks aimed at Americans were occurring. Four explosions were set off by the VC during January and February 1964. The biggest was the bombing of the Kinh Do movie theater in Saigon, killing three Americans and wounding 32.[4]

Serving with World Evangelism Crusade (WEC), Roy and Daphne Spraggett lived near the Demilitarized Zone in a place called Cam Phu. On January 26, 1964, after a day of church

---

[4] This, and other facts in this section are found in *By Life or By Death* (Hefley, 1969).

services, they and their two-year-old daughter went to bed. Terrorists snuck in and placed a bomb in their house while they were asleep.

Years later Betty shared with her children:

During the war I was calm because I knew that I was exactly where I was supposed to be. That helped me all the time. There was just one time when we lived in Kontum right near the jungle when I was overcome with worry. Kathy was probably around one and a half.

There was this missionary couple that worked up toward Danang. They were asleep in their house one night with their little girl who was almost the same age as Kathy. The VC came and put an explosive device in the little girl's room. But that night she was sick so she was in bed with her parents. Suddenly an explosive blew up her bed. It blew clear to the ceiling. But she was alive.

After that, I was constantly afraid that was going to happen to us. Just beyond the two or three houses between our house and the edge of the village was an area overgrown with tall weeds, bushes and trees. It was the perfect place for the enemy to sneak into the village at night and do the same thing to us.

We had several windows. They didn't have glass in them, but had wooden shutters with slits. Every day before dusk I would go through the house making sure that every shutter was closed tight and latched. I was consumed by fear—a very miserable existence. When I cried out to the Lord for help, He drew Psalm 56:3-4 to my mind, "What time I am afraid, I will trust in the Lord." That broke the whole cycle of worry, and I was fine after that. People often wonder how we faced what we faced. It was the grace of God making it possible.

UNSTOPPABLE!

By 1964 the U.S. military personnel in Viet Nam numbered around 20,000. The Communists who infiltrated down from the north into South Viet Nam increased from 20,000 to 165,000 and continued to build their forces.

Nearly six years had elapsed since John and Betty had left home. In March 1964 the Bankers left for furlough in the U.S. John invested a portion of this time studying linguistics at Hartford University in Connecticut. He and Betty also went to Mexico to attend a Bible translation workshop led by John Beekman.

While studying in Connecticut, the Bankers were blessed by Pastor Hervey Taber and his wife, Shirley, who were planting a church in Ellington. Every Sunday morning Pastor Taber picked up the Banker family for church. After the service they ate dinner in the Taber home. Shirley's mother, whom the Bankers affectionately called Grammy Payton, cooked a scrumptious meal each week, after which she and Betty washed dishes together. Grammy became a faithful prayer warrior on their behalf, and the Bankers became the first of many missionaries the Ellington Wesleyan Church prayed for and supported financially.

On November 15, 1964, John wrote:

Today the Taber family came to our place for dinner. We had a nice time. They are a very nice family and have helped us out a lot. And Tommy really likes Mark, the little boy of theirs that is about his age.

UNSTOPPABLE!

The Bankers returned to Viet Nam a year and a half later with two "MAs": John, with an M.A. in Linguistics, and Betty with an M.A. in the form of a beautiful baby girl, Mary Alice.

With their home assignment drawing to a close, the Bankers traveled to Canada to see Betty's family. During Kathy's short life, she had been plagued by recurring urinary tract infections with regularly spiking fevers. John took Kathy to a urologist at the University of Alberta Hospital in Edmonton. The doctor found that her urethra was too small to function properly and performed an operation to stretch it. He told John this might take care of the problem, but it could re-occur.

For several months Kathy was fine, but then after they returned to Viet Nam in late 1965, the high fevers returned. John and Betty were very thankful for a Catholic hospital in the central highlands with a very dedicated American doctor. She mainly served the medical needs of the Montagnard peoples but was always happy to care for the needs of the missionaries.

UNSTOPPABLE!

Little Tommy, Kathy and Mary Alice, along with their parents, adjusted back to life in Viet Nam again. At first, all five-year-old Tommy could talk about was the Viet Cong. He had never mentioned them before, but all during the Bankers' furlough in the U.S he had heard the adult discussions about the war as well as bits and pieces of the news broadcasts. Nearly a week back in Viet Nam, he stopped talking about the Viet Cong and stopped worrying about them.

One Friday night a Christian U.S. serviceman who worked on helicopter engines came for supper. He brought Tommy a model airplane, a B-36. John hung it from the ceiling in Tommy's room. Tommy loved airplanes; with an airport a mile away and two helicopter landing pads just a few hundred yards away, aircraft flew overhead all day long, giving Tommy lots of opportunities to learn about them. Tommy begged to have his daddy read the encyclopedia section on airplanes almost every day.

John wrote home to his parents from Kontum:

> This week was an exciting week. First the big C-130 transports planes started coming in one after another. This kept up for about three days. Twenty-seven came in the first day and for the next two days there were more than that each day and into the night.
>
> Then we started seeing a lot of American soldiers around with jeeps and trucks. Then they started moving them from here to out west of here near the Laos border by helicopter. There were a lot of small helicopters and also some big ones called Chinooks.

UNSTOPPABLE!

Then they brought some big artillery pieces to the field down the road a bit. The Chinooks came down, picked up troops and then hovered over a big gun while a fellow got up and attached it to the Chinook and then they attached another load below that.

Then better yet, in came the flying crane helicopter which is really a monstrosity. It picked up an even bigger gun yet. You can imagine that Tommy was pretty excited and Kathy too.

In January 1966, a newspaper article with a picture and story of Tommy appeared in "The Observer," a U.S. Army publication in Viet Nam. The man who came to interview Tommy was part of a syndicate which represented hundreds of newspapers so the story came out in a number of newspapers across the United States. Again, in February 1967, an excerpt from the Rochester Democrat and Chronicle read:

> Like every other imaginative, adventurous 6-year-old, towheaded Tommy Banker likes to play war. Only for Tommy it's not make-believe. It's armed troops, nearby gunfire, cordite and chopper chatter.
>
> So, it is each day the lad rushes directly from his schoolwork to more serious pursuits-that of helping the Allies win the war. First thing is to find a helmet. A cap is too soft. A pail is too big. A mixing bowl, perfect. Next, he needs a gun. Two sticks will do it.
>
> Tommy crouches low in his back yard. He sees something suspicious by the fence. He shuffles quietly to the side of the house. He stops. He looks around. Then he sneaks along the open ground. He aims his stick. "Bam, bam!"

UNSTOPPABLE!

And every chicken runs for cover. Tommy Banker has been battling his enemies for most of his life.

He doesn't mind, however. In truth, this, not America, is his home...The GIs always give him a salute, feel his muscles, show him their guns and present him with dogface honorariums [fatigue caps, parachutes, badges, etc.]. It's a good life for a 6-year old. Until the school bell rings, anyway.

War No Make-Believe for Tommy, 6 — Tiede in Vietnam

For Tommy's sixth birthday an MP took him on a tour of the Army camp and airbase, which included climbing into several airplanes. [Years later in Nha Trang, when Tommy was 13, he and several of his friends were taken on a flight in a little Air America Beechcraft plane. Each took turns flying the plane. Tom had the exciting experience of flying the plane as it took off.]

In 1966 John and Betty were still living in Kontum. While waiting for Om to come from Pleiku so they could work together on Acts, John applied what he had learned on furlough to revise the initial translation of Mark's Gospel.

Now better equipped to lead translation workshops, John delighted to share his training with newer translation teams. He gave translation orientation to Nancy Costello and helped her with the translation of Bible stories for the Katu people. Ken Smith was also translating the Life of Christ Bible stories into the Sedang language. Dwight Gradin was translating the same stories into the Jeh language.

Three times a week John led seminars on translation problems and techniques, then looked over the work of these three translation teams and suggested improvements. The Life of Christ selections included stories of the birth of Jesus and some of Jesus' miracles, then finished with Jesus' trial, crucifixion and resurrection. After the workshop, John checked the Gospel of Mark which Dave and Dottie Thomas had translated into the Chrau language. He really enjoyed this experience as a consultant.

The Bankers next project was to produce several textbooks for Bahnar schools and thus promote literacy and the capability of reading God's Word. Eventually Om was able to come for a short visit, but he was now helping an American man who worked with the Viet Nam Christian Service cultivating an experimental garden. John needed to look for another Bahnar translator. Gail Fleming with the C&MA came to Kontum and agreed to look for a Bahnar or two who could come help.

UNSTOPPABLE!

Helping Others in Times of Need (1965-66)

In 1966 the Bankers returned to Saigon to fill in, once again, in various roles while their colleagues were taking their furloughs or on shorter trips to their home countries. Betty served as group house manager; John was the buyer as well as being involved in government relations and other positions of leadership.

About this time the Ministry of Ethnic Minorities asked the Bankers, and their colleagues trained in linguistics, to create a major multilingual education program for the minority peoples of Viet Nam. Because the children from minority language communities were not fluent in Vietnamese they were failing in school. The Bankers and others were to produce programs and materials to help these minority people to succeed in school.

With their colleagues, the Bankers received training from Dr. Sarah Gutchinsky, an international literacy specialist [in photo]. A major breakthrough occurred when she devised a method of focused syllable drills to help people from these languages of Viet Nam learn to read.

John, Betty and their Bahnar counterparts began producing Bahnar primers, textbooks, and teacher education manuals. To produce these educational materials, the Bankers worked with a Catholic man from the Bahnar

UNSTOPPABLE!

Kontum dialect as well as others. The government agency assisted in other ways, mimeographing and stapling the printed materials. The materials were distributed to 18 public schools in the central highlands.

The program began with teaching minority children to read in their mother tongue. Each year the amount of Vietnamese in the primers was gradually increased so that by the end of the program students could read in their mother tongue as well as Vietnamese.

As the Bankers also trained Bahnar adults to teach Bahnar children how to read, the program began to spread across the central highlands.

The Pleiku Training Center, where Bankers and others provided this training, was located on one hilltop. Not far away on a neighboring hilltop stood a military outpost and the airstrip on yet another. The airstrip and the outpost were targets for enemy mortars. Mortar shells at times missed their targets and landed close to the Training Center, disrupting the trainees' studies.

As the literacy program progressed, John reported to his director:

> The government inspector is thinking that these workshops were valuable enough that Vietnamese teachers could profit from them and so invited 15 Vietnamese teachers to the Bahnar one here.

> It [the literacy program] is beginning to take hold in the schools. We must do our part to see that the program is a success. We don't want it to be a failure. I think we have to get away from the idea that our part is to produce the

materials only, like an academic exercise. We have to have that contact with the officials and teachers too...If we have sold the program to the government then we cannot let them down now.

Many benefits were realized from this program among the Montagnard peoples. High dropout rates of first-year students decreased sharply, down from 90 percent. Now children began to complete a grade in a year rather than taking two to three. Parents began to believe it worthwhile to send their children to school. Up to this point mainly boys attended; with the success of the new program, parents now sent their girls to school also. This led to improvement in the socioeconomic situation of the communities and the ability to read the translated scriptures.

The national leaders of the Bureau of Ethnic Minorities in Saigon were very pleased with the success of the program and those involved in it. "If there are other Christian young people who want to become literacy workers, have them go to the Pleiku Training Center," they said. "We have seen that it is the Christian young people who are motivated to work without reward."

UNSTOPPABLE!

One of the men who helped the Bankers in this major multilingual education project stayed with them. However, because there was no spare space in the missionary group house, he ended up sharing their bedroom. A wardrobe and draped bedspreads divided the room into two.

The missionaries had been searching without success to find a place with more space. John wrote home, "This house is so crowded with people and things that it is really funny."

The Bankers remained engaged in many projects. Bill Smalley from the Bible Society helped John check the Gospel of Mark in the Bahnar language. Bill suggested John learn more about how the logical connections between sentences and ideas function in Bahnar. Increased understanding of Bahnar culture was also essential for producing translated scripture that could be understood accurately.

About this time the war was heating up with more nations becoming officially involved. Some nights the Bankers lay in bed in the missionary group house watching rockets light up the sky. One night they heard a missionary wife in the next room crying.

John wrote home: "Saigon seems to have quieted down. We pray that it might stay that way. The Lord takes care of His children."

In early 1966 John wrote home:

> Although it may seem to people outside Viet Nam that the door is almost closed, we are having opportunities now that we have never had before. Among the Jeh tribe many people have had to leave their homes to flee to more secure places. Uprooted from their old

surroundings, they have also been forced to change some of their religious practices because they don't fit with the new situations they are in. Many of them are turning to Protestant Christianity. Let's pray they will not just take on another religion but really be born again.

I just got back from the last meeting of an evangelistic crusade that was held this last week in the soccer stadium here. There were about 5,000 people there tonight. They said that over 700 Vietnamese had gone forward during the meetings. We are praising the Lord for his working here.

The pastor of the International church held meetings this past week for a U.S. army unit outside Saigon and 60 people accepted Christ. So you see God is at work here.

Some members of the Venture for Victory Basketball team which tour the Orient playing basketball and witnessing for Christ were speakers at the service. It was very good.

Bob Reed in Phu Bon stated:

There can be no doubt that this is a time of awesome upheaval in Viet Nam, a time of terrible heartache, uncertainty and fear for her people. However, God is fashioning from the chaos of human suffering a vital and shining image of faith, and is daily opening up new avenues to communicate that faith to others.

Dave Frazier, a C&MA missionary who worked closely with the Bankers, said:

I believe Viet Nam is on the brink of a great awakening, a great harvest. Never...has the Church had such opportunity.

UNSTOPPABLE!

Bob Henry from Dalat echoed a similar sentiment when he said:

> Pioneer missionaries found the Vietnamese satisfied in their spiritual darkness. This is no longer the case...The whirlwind of war has brought forth confusion of mind and restlessness of soul. This is our unique opportunity to present the Prince of Peace to this troubled sea of war-weary humanity.[5]

As the war escalated, so did the suffering. More than a million refugees and an increasing number of injured, hungry and ill-clothed due to war now filled the country. Relief efforts poured in from abroad. By 1966 some 26 relief organizations, mostly religious and mostly from the U.S. were operating.

Many missionaries from various organizations served in the central highland cities of Dalat, Ban Me Thuot, Kontum and Pleiku. Missionaries Gordon and Laura Smith opened a leprosy rehabilitation center, two orphanages and a chapel for 300 children. Local U.S. GIs generously provided money to build the chapel. They also created a 50-pound brass cross constructed from used shell casings which they set up behind the pulpit.

Servicemen from each of the American military units engaged in some type of civic action project. They helped build schools and playgrounds and provided clothes and other supplies. One unit donated a large-print typewriter and

---

[5] These three quotes and other facts in this section are found in *By Life or By Death* (Hefley, 1969).

mimeograph machine to help one ethnic minority people group learn to read.

A Vietnamese Catholic nun who was the head of the largest private school and orphanage in the city of Danang said, "When the Americans leave, it will be the schools and orphanages that will feel the greatest loss. They have done so much to help."

A missionary newsletter reported:

> There is a stream of military men, from privates to colonels, coming almost daily to the orphanage with food or clothing and asking, "What can I do?" Almost every unit has some special project that is closest to their hearts and they are jealous of it. One AMTRAC unit is helping the missionaries to establish a medical center.
>
> If there is any one thing that has characterized our half a million [military] men in Viet Nam in 1967, it has been the involvement of thousands of them in feeding the hungry, caring for the children by finding homes or an orphanage for them, bringing gallons of milk and tubs of ice cream to the orphanages, working with the lepers, building churches, bulldozing locations for buildings and putting in electric lights...God bless them for having a heart for the people around them.[6]

During 1965 the Communist forces infiltrated the Ban Me Thuot, Pleiku and Kontum area. The surrounding jungle swarmed with enemy soldiers constantly on the move. It almost looked as if the Bahnar area would be completely

---

[6] Taken from *United World Mission Reports (1968). One Year Later in Viet Nam: More of Everything in Sixty-Seven* by Sidney Correll.

overrun. The fledgling Bahnar church was in great danger. Into this tension arrived the American combat troops—the First Cavalry and the 4th Division.

With their arrival, things quieted down and evangelism in Bahnar villages could continue. A young Bahnar man named Yohansi became a strong Christian. As an interpreter in the evangelical clinic he began witnessing to the many Bahnar people who came for treatment.

Around this time a new linguistic center was built in Kontum. The land for the center was a gift from the Vietnamese government because of missionaries' diligent efforts to educate the minority peoples. Attendees trained in three-month workshops in language analysis, translation and literacy principles.

The new linguistic center in Kontum

The Alliance and WEC missionaries who worked with minority people groups also joined in these workshops. The literacy materials produced were used by the missionaries, the Vietnamese government, and U.S. AID.

UNSTOPPABLE!

By July 1966 the Bankers, together with their Bahnar coworkers, finished a little over 2,000 primers for the start of the multilingual education program among the Bahnar.

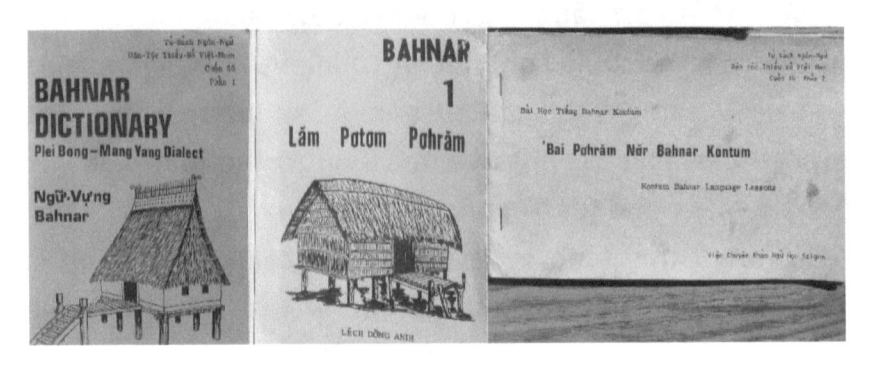

John flew on a C-46 Air America flight up to Kontum where he distributed the materials to schools and the Department of Education. He returned to Saigon on an Air Force C-130, and later returned once again to Kontum to check on how the program was going.

By autumn of 1966 the Bankers completed their various group-service roles in Saigon and returned to Kontum. John led a translation workshop for other teams doing Bible translation.

They were hoping that Om, who had previously helped with the translation of Mark, could come assist with Acts. However, by now Om had joined the South Vietnamese Army. The Bankers also hoped to relocate to Pleiku to spend full time in translating the Bible for the Bahnar people. A small, but growing Bahnar church was flourishing, and John and Betty were looking forward to fellowshipping with them.

UNSTOPPABLE!

Family (1966-67)

The missionary families in Kontum were regularly invited to celebrate Thanksgiving and other holidays at MAC-V (the American Military Assistance Command-Viet Nam), the U.S. military post outside Kontum. They enjoyed all kinds of goodies they could never get otherwise. Loaded plates of turkey, ham, pumpkin pie, mincemeat pie, apples, oranges and nuts filled the tables. After Thanksgiving dinner short cartoons for the children were shown, to which Vietnamese children were also invited.

Since birth, Kathy Banker had been sick with recurring fevers and infections, particularly urinary tract infections. John and Betty wrote home frequently to ask for prayer for their now four-year-old daughter:

> Kathy is sick today with a fever. She may have the same trouble that she had when we were home. We are thankful there are American doctors and medics here, and also a Swiss medic team. We plan to take her to the U.S. army dispensary tomorrow. Please pray for her that she may be healthy and may not have a lot of trouble.

They also wrote to help their parents participate in what was happening in their grandchildren's lives:

> Mary Alice is growing as sweet as she can be. She is more like Tommy in disposition. She is learning to talk. When she says the blessing, her prayer goes like this, "Thank you Daddy, Mommy, Tommy, Kathy, food."

> Right now she [Mary Alice] is pulling the kitty by the tail. She likes all kinds of animals. The little lizards climb on the

UNSTOPPABLE!

walls and ceiling and she thinks that they are quite exciting. They walk on the ceiling and hardly ever fall off. They don't bother people at all but catch a lot of insects.

Tommy and Kathy love Jesus and like to sing hymns and choruses and read Bible stories. Tommy is a very good boy most of the time. Kathy is at the mischievous age. Kathy is a tomboy—always climbing and tumbling around. But she is also very girlish and ladylike at other times. She loves fancy, frilly clothes, and is particular about how her hair looks. She is such a contradiction to herself at times.

Sometimes John's love of his home in Upstate New York came through in his letters. He could see the home he loved reflected in the central highlands of Viet Nam. He wrote:

To the west there is a mountain that looks a lot like Lyon Mountain and foothills that look like the hills above West Plattsburgh. And then looking south there is a valley and then on the other side the area looks a lot like the Beckwith St. area as we can see it from home. To the north again there are no hills that we can see from here so that is like home, too. However, to the southeast there are some mountains that are quite close, which is different from home. They are not very high, though. And north of the mountain that looks like Lyon mountain, there is a rather tall peaked one.

UNSTOPPABLE!

The Bankers lived on the other side of town from the airport and from where most of the military were stationed. The military were the main targets for Viet Cong mortar attacks. At that time Kontum had a population of over 50,000.

Another workshop was planned for the later part of 1967 for all those doing Bible translation. John appreciated the teamwork taking place. Gail Fleming with the C&MA was also doing some translation for the Bahnar to use in their church services. He translated Luke 15 as well as John 18 and 20 and then sent it to John to look over.

John wrote home:

> Gail Fleming and I have been checking through the Bible translation that he has been doing. It is a Bible Overview booklet with the scripture from the whole Bible telling the gospel story, about 40 pages long.

Kontum was home to many Catholic institutions. A Catholic school for preparing Montagnard boys for lay ministry was situated behind the Bankers' home. Across the street stood a home for priests and another school was down the main street nearby, along with a large church, orphanage and nunnery. The Bahnar man working with the Bankers to produce the teachers' guides for the multilingual education program had been an orphan who was raised by the Catholic church.

By mid-1967, John and Betty were serving their fellow missionaries in yet a new role. More children from missionary families were becoming school age so the group desired to start a small school. Behind the Banker house stood a one-room building that they used for a school.

By the beginning of the new academic year, three children came to live with the Bankers in order to go to school; John and Betty, served as dorm parents. Their extended family now included three boys and three girls. Betty wrote home:

> I wonder what it will be like to have 3 six-year-old boys in the house...I'm kind of looking forward to it. It will be fun to just be mommy full time for a change.

[Cindy Blood, Tommy, Jeff Blood, Kathy, Larry Watson, Benny Lee]

John wrote home:

Dave and Doris and Jeffrey [Blood] came up this week since the house was too crowded in Saigon.

So, Tommy has been having fun staying with Jeffrey, including watching the tanks and trucks go by and the helicopters in the air. It seems like every 2 or 3 months some combat unit—like the 1st Cavalry or 101st Airborne comes up for a few weeks.

UNSTOPPABLE!

There is a chaplain here with the 1st Cavalry who graduated from Houghton in the 1940s. He is a very good man. He arranged for some of the soldiers to help us out a little getting ready for our school. They have made a couple of bookshelves and are making a bulletin board for the school.

Last week the 1st Cavalry brought us two big truckloads of sand which we have been using for fill for our yard, which gets very muddy, since it is lower than everything around it.

David Standing, a fellow missionary, built a play house right next to the school. Plastic windows were a lot cheaper than glass, so some were made for the school. The frames were made at a carpenter shop; then plastic was bought and stapled on to the frames.

No electricity served that part of the town. The Bankers used gas lanterns that would get dim and have to be pumped up periodically to keep them going. Eventually the Bankers were able to get three electric lights installed; one each in the living-dining room, bathroom and master bedroom. The kitchen and two children's bedrooms remained without electrical illumination.

Betty was very busy taking care of six children. Every night each needed to bathe and get ready for bed. It was no small task to put up six mosquito nets each night to keep from being eaten by mosquitoes.

In September of that year, Betty added yet another job when the missionaries' two-week-conference began. As head of the kitchen, Betty was in charge of supervising each meal and all the needed preparation. During the conference several children who had been living with the Bankers stayed with their parents who were attending the meetings in town.

After the conference John planned to head for Pleiku to find someone to help him with translation. He was delayed, however, because Kathy became sick again the day before he intended to leave. They took her over to Doctor Smith who worked at the Catholic hospital. After more medication, Kathy felt better the next day, but she still wasn't strong.

John left for Pleiku by helicopter the next morning. Om, now married and the father of a 16-month-old boy, was very excited to see his friend. When John told Om the Bankers were hoping to move back to Pleiku the following year, Om offered to build them a house right next to his own. When John arrived back in Kontum, Tommy was excited about the helicopter rides and wanted to hear all about them.

For the time being, the Bankers still needed to remain in Kontum. While John waited for a Bahnar to come work with him full time on Bible translation, he assisted other ethnic minorities by developing literacy manuals to aid them in learning how to read their own languages. One was Jarai, the largest ethnic group in South Viet Nam, with a population estimated as high as 130,000 people.

UNSTOPPABLE!

At the end of October, one of John's long-desired prayers was answered. The Fraziers (serving with the C&MA) brought a new Bahnar helper named He'i from Pleiku to Kontum. Only about 20 years of age and married, with a little girl about a year old, He'i was one of the lay leaders in his village. God had preserved his life when, just a few months previously, He'i had been captured with others in his village and taken to the mountains. Planes flying overhead discovered their captors in the highlands and attacked the kidnappers. He'i and the other captives took the opportunity to flee.

When He'i and John began to work together, He'i wanted to translate a hymn into his language. They worked together to translate a couple verses of *When I Survey the Wondrous Cross*. When He'i took the song home, the Bahnar people sang it and found a new love: singing praise to the Lord in their own language!

Soon John and He'i had translated more than 20 hymns. They also began translating the Book of Acts. By the year's end John and He'i had finished the first draft of 24 chapters of Acts.

UNSTOPPABLE!

The kids really enjoyed He'i too. He made objects for them out of bamboo and wood. He liked to play games; sometimes he would fold his eyelids up and chase the kids while they ran away in mock terror.

In late October Betty planned a Halloween party. She was busy making costumes for each of the children. With excitement they went to the American military compound to do their trick-or-treating.

The enjoyment was not just one-sided. The soldiers had fun too, many of them missing their own families back home.

On November 21, 1967 John wrote home:

> We were told twice on the same day this week that Kontum is the safest or most secure province in the country, once by an American captain, the other time by a Vietnamese official. We are thankful to the Lord for this.
>
> We have been invited out to the American post for Thanksgiving. The chaplain came up and invited us down the other day. I am sure they will have a very good meal...We have a lot of things to be thankful for.

The missionaries also celebrated a Thanksgiving dinner at their linguistic center. Three turkeys had been brought up from the PX in Saigon. One of the American military units in Kontum gave them a 13-pound turkey plus six boxes of apples, oranges, and lemons. The Bankers were able to bring two boxes back to their little school.

John, who grew up on an apple orchard, said:

> We have never had so many apples in Viet Nam. We have them stored in our bedroom and it really smells nice!

UNSTOPPABLE!

Tet – The Chinese New Year of 1968

In January 1968, an Anthropology workshop was held at the linguistic center led by Marilyn Gregerson. John wanted to learn more of the Bahnar beliefs and worldview. He studied words the Bahnar used for judging legal cases because this terminology occurred repeatedly in the Book of Acts, which he was translating at that time. Among other things, he needed to discover the Bahnar words for "accuse" and "defend."

John and He'i finished translating the first draft of Acts in January. Several other Bahnar who were staying at the linguistic center came to help. To John's joy, one of the young men named Tuwari asked Jesus into his heart and life. He'i began to disciple him.

On January 25, 1968 John wrote home:

> The day after tomorrow is Tet, the Vietnamese New Year. Like usual we will be making little gifts of cookies and candy for some of our friends among the Vietnamese.
>
> I'll tell you a secret. We are expecting another addition to our family around about the first part of September, the Lord willing.

As Tet, the Chinese Lunar New Year, was approaching people were getting ready to celebrate. This special holiday is a time for wishing one another wealth, happiness, and long life.

The Communists were also getting ready—but for something very different. They began passing out propaganda leaflets using words like "time opportunity," "general uprising," and "general offensive."

In the time leading up to Tet, an "uprising committee" had been formed to help with the military take-over of cities and towns across Viet Nam. The Communist-led Tet attacks began in Quang Tri, which was located near the DMZ line, and were to be carried out all the way to the island of Phu Quoc located near the Delta in the very southern part of the country. Some VC wore peasant clothes and South Vietnamese army uniforms they took from laundry shops. Others wore North Vietnamese uniforms. They came as if out of thin air, intent on bringing death and destruction to soldiers, civilians, Buddhists, and Christians.

Monday, January 29 was a very busy day for the Bankers as they too prepared to celebrate Tet the following day. Most of the day was spent joyfully baking cakes, cookies, brownies and other specialty food, then wrapping them and delivering the goodies along with greeting cards to their Vietnamese friends. Seventeen homes were blessed by the gifts, so it was almost 11pm when they dropped exhausted into bed.

At midnight the Chinese New Year was greeted with loud firecrackers. John and Betty awakened, while the five children continued sleeping. By 12:30am the celebratory noise quieted down and they drifted off to sleep again.

Two hours later they were abruptly reawakened, this time by the sounds of mortars and rockets. This was serious!

John and Betty quickly got up, woke the children and led them to the shower area of the bathroom. This was the most protected area of the house, with brick walls extending to the ceiling on three sides and about six feet high on the fourth side. John's project of putting a sandbag roof on the shower and partially blocking the doorway with sandbags for use as a bunker was not yet finished; only a framework was in place. For immediate protection, the Bankers with their extra schoolchildren now crouched in the small shower.

In the previous months the few attacks at the airport and the American army bases had ended quickly. But this time was different. The noise from the attack would never stop, it seemed. Betty distracted the children by encouraging them to think of Bible verses that started with every letter of the alphabet.

The narrow space was uncomfortable for seven people to squeeze into for hours. Toward morning, six-year-old Larry Watson couldn't stand it anymore, so John followed him out into the hall and slept with him there. That gave more room for Cindy Blood, Tommy, Kathy, and Mary Alice who then were able to lie down and most fell asleep. Betty stood so as to give the children as much space as possible.

The loud attack continued all through the night. When morning dawned, John moved with the boys into their room; Betty went with the girls into their room to sleep. The sound of mortars and rockets continued, but wasn't close by.

Prior to the Tet celebration, Stan Smith, another missionary in Kontum, had seen signs that trouble might be approaching. The Viet Cong had distributed propaganda leaflets in the market area, boasting they would have their own celebration in the highland city of Kontum.

Stan's concern increased when the U.S. 173rd Airborne left Kontum for an area of fierce fighting. Now the Viet Cong could take advantage of the decreased military presence. With this trouble brewing, Stan and his wife Ginny headed for Da Nang.

However, many missionary families remained in Kontum for a literacy workshop which followed the Anthropology workshop at the linguistic center. Participants included the Ernest Lees, Kenneth Gregersons, James Coopers, Dave Bloods, Eugenia Johnston, Pat Bonnell, Judy Wallace, and Pat Cohen. Carolyn Miller was also there with her preschool age children. Other families participating were the Richard Phillips (C&MA who worked in Ban Me Thuot) and the Oliver Trebilcos (WEC missionaries to an ethnic group south of Da Nang). Language assistants from the various languages were also involved.

While the Bankers had been busy baking and cooking specialty items to share with their friends and neighbors, Monday of Tet week was like any other day for those involved in the literacy workshop. Participants produced primers in the various minority languages.

At the end of the day, Coopers, Gregersons and Lees left for their homes several miles away. The Bankers remained in their home, also across town from the linguistic center.

UNSTOPPABLE!

At 2:30am mortar and machine gun fire brought everyone staying at the linguistic center out of their beds. The adults kept a calm exterior as they hurried the children outside into bunkers prepared for such an occasion. Dug into the ground, the bunkers' entrances were rimmed with protective sandbags. For some, this was a new experience.

The Dave Blood family, Carolyn Miller with her children, and Eugenia Johnston climbed down into the shared bunker behind their living quarters.

Suddenly two legs appeared in the bunker entrance! Fear of a Viet Cong grenade gripped them.

In a moment they saw...Pat Cohen! He had entered his own little bunker behind his apartment, but the sandbags started falling in on him. Instead of taking the risk of being buried under a crumbling bunker he came to join his colleagues.

Due to the tenseness of the situation, the children found it hard to sleep. One kept saying, "Oh, I hope the VC don't get us."

Eugenia Johnston said sternly, "Will you be quiet and let the adults do the worrying!"

UNSTOPPABLE!

The missionaries prayed together, then "Uncle" Pat Cohen began story time. "Goldilocks lay fast asleep when suddenly…."

A dragon roared, but not a fairytale one. "Puff the Magic Dragon" (a U.S. C-47 airplane with powerful machine guns that could fire thousands of rounds per minute) zoomed overhead, blasting a river of lead at the Viet Cong entrenchments only a few hundred yards away. Following close behind the C-47, helicopter gunships blasted rockets on enemy positions.

The ear-splitting, nerve-wracking night stretched long hours. But morning brought calm to the hostilities, so the missionaries cautiously climbed out of their bunkers.

After breakfast, the children went to sleep in their own beds. Amazingly their homes and property suffered no damage, and everyone at the linguistic center was safe and sound.

Their next concern was whether the four missionary families living in town had survived the night. There was no way to contact the Bankers, Coopers, Gregersons, and Lees to find out.

The North Vietnamese Army (NVA) now was entrenched in the hospital grounds and other strategic places in the city from where they launched their mortars. By noon on Tuesday, the Chinese New Year's Day, the Communists came against the airfield in a ground attack—only three blocks from the Coopers' home.

UNSTOPPABLE!

In response, U.S. helicopter gunships swarmed the sky overhead, protecting the airfield. The battle quieted down about 2pm, but three hours later intensified again. During the attack the Coopers jumped into their bunker behind their house.

On Monday night the Gregersons had also heard ammunition blasting. The sounds of celebration soon turned into the deafening noise of battle. The NVA set up a machine gun near their yard from which they fired into the American Special Forces base about a half block away.

When the Gregersons realized a battle was raging outside their door they quickly moved to the makeshift bunker inside the house. Two walls of the house formed two sides of the bunker and sandbags the other two sides.

After the fighting died down in the morning, a Buddhist monk from the temple next door came over. He had become friends with Ken through playing basketball together in Gregersons' front yard. He gave them a running commentary of the battle while they took cover inside.

The Gregersons also had another visitor, the daughter of the Vietnamese pastor who lived down the road. She told Ken and Marilyn that the VC had come to her house the night before. Seeing a vehicle outside their house, the soldiers had shouted at them to come out and sprayed bullets at their house. The pastor and his family held their breath as they kept low and hid under beds. To their great relief the soldiers moved on.

UNSTOPPABLE!

The next morning the pastor's daughter slipped over to Gregersons to beg them to remove the vehicle. Carefully, Ken made his way to the pastor's house. Parked there was Stan Smith's Land Rover—a much-needed provision for escape! Ken drove it home; his family piled into the vehicle and they drove straight to the U.S. Special Forces base.

The Gregersons were the first of the missionary families to reach the base and Camp MAC-V adjacent to it. Ken quickly informed the commander of the desperate plight of his fellow missionaries.

The busy commander sent Ken outside where the helicopters were coming and going, flying in ammunition and supplies from Pleiku to stock the bases for coming attacks. [The smaller bases were located in Kontum and the larger ones in Pleiku.] Then He instructed, "Stand there and try to signal to the helicopters. One of them may be able to fly to the linguistic center and rescue your friends!"

Ken and the chaplain stood outside from early afternoon till 5:00pm. It was getting close to supper time before they were able to catch the eye of a helicopter pilot to go to the rescue.

Meanwhile, Tuesday was passing slowly back at the linguistic center. Fighting continued sporadically throughout the day. The children slept.

Suddenly a bullet shot through the wall about eighteen inches from Richard Philip's head, passed through the wall, then lodged in the kitchen door. Carolyn Miller, recently evacuated from Khe Sanh, mentioned that it might be a good idea to pack suitcases in case the missionaries needed to evacuate suddenly. The others agreed and packed some belongings but otherwise life went on as normal.

Later that afternoon the women were preparing supper when the noise of a loud roaring sounded outside. An American soldier rushed in, exclaiming, "The VC and NVA are all over the place. You can't use the road to get to our base. There are too many snipers. Grab what you can and get in the chopper!"

The women quickly turned off the stoves, leaving the hot food behind. Everyone rushed to climb into the helicopter. Eugenia Fuller and the Miller children piled on with the rest. As their mother, Carolyn, began to board, the helicopter was declared full. There was no more room!

In alarm, Eugenia grabbed Carolyn to pull her on board but to no avail; no space remained. The helicopter took off in a cloud of dust, leaving behind Carolyn and the others.

But it wasn't long before the distinctive chop of whirring rotors sounded again. Carolyn, relieved and thankful, piled aboard with the others. The helicopter whisked them over the barbed wire fences, heading with determination to the MAC-V compound nearby, where it eased its way down and safely deposited them within the sandbagged walls. The missionaries climbed off one by one. The soldiers, though tired and worn from battle, kindly welcomed them in to find refuge on the base.

The rescued missionaries were relieved to see the Gregersons had already arrived. But the other missionary

UNSTOPPABLE!

families living in Kontum had not yet made it to safety. Dave Blood expressed his concern to the commanding officer, "Major, we have three more families still out there."

The officer replied. "I'm sorry, but we didn't know where they lived until Mr. Gregerson arrived. Those families are too close to the fighting. A chopper or armored vehicle would just get shot up."

As the light of day faded into night, Army Chaplain Marvin advised the arrivals to spend the night in two well-built concrete bunkers to avoid the dangers of running from the rooms to the bunkers at night. [Doris Blood would later write: "The Name of the Lord was to be the shelter for these folk for the next two nights."]

The missionaries crowded into the bunkers. Cots for sleeping could only be found for one in ten.

And now, the first major wave of Communist ground troops attacked. The MAC-V defenders, vastly outnumbered, fought back. The noise of battle was deafening.

The missionaries prayed. "Uncle" Pat Cohen again told stories to the children.

Throughout the long night, the Communists came in wave after wave of unrelenting suicidal attacks. As dawn broke the NVA retreated again to regroup and care for their wounded.

On Wednesday morning some of the missionaries walked around the perimeter of the base with the soldiers. Uniformed North Vietnamese dead bodies lay all over the ground. A sergeant said with regret, "It was either them or us."

Bodies of North Vietnamese soldiers were also found strewn here and there at the linguistic center. The number of the dead equaled the number of the missionaries evacuated from the center the evening before.

The Bankers were still in their house on the outskirts of Kontum. At about 8am on Tuesday morning, John called Betty into the hallway to tell her some of their Bahnar friends had just come by. They were fleeing, carrying their belongings on their backs. They informed John that the Viet Cong were on their way through town and had now arrived at the market, about a half mile away.

John invited their Bahnar friends to stay in the school room. However, they were heading for the edge of town which was only a few hundred yards behind the Bankers' home. There they could disappear into the fields and jungle.

After their friends' departure, John and Betty carried the dining table into the girls' bedroom, pushing it into the corner against two walls. They grabbed sandbags from the bathroom and laid them on top and along one side of the table. Two mattresses were placed on top of the sandbags and one under the table. The window was covered with a blanket.

They took the children from their beds and placed them on the mattress under the table. John and Betty crawled under the table with the children. Kathy and Mary Alice continued to sleep for another hour or so.

UNSTOPPABLE!

When the children awoke, John and Betty tried to keep them as quiet as possible to avoid being heard by the Viet Cong if they came that way. They told the children stories and played games. Once again, they took turns thinking of Bible verses that started with every letter of the alphabet.

John and Betty also talked about what the Lord Jesus meant to the children individually. They wanted to be sure each child was ready to meet the Lord at any moment since this was a very real possibility. When the children became hungry and thirsty, John went to the kitchen and returned with water and bread along with a can for relieving themselves.

About noon He'i came to the window and called John, who went to the door. He'i informed John things had calmed down and they could now exit their indoor bunker. So they let the kids out but remained inside the house with the curtains shut.

Not knowing when they would again have a chance to have another square meal, John and Betty prepared a roast dinner and boiled a supply of drinking water. They packed suitcases in case they needed to evacuate quickly.

John and the boys moved a second table into the girl's bedroom to enlarge the "bunker." Thankfully, Pat Cohen had provided a good supply of sandbags after hearing rumors of possible attacks on Kontum; these were stacked atop and along the sides of the table. Another mattress and pillows were placed underneath. They also brought food, water, and snacks into the room, in case they needed to hunker down for an extended time.

By late afternoon the sounds of war started up again. The Viet Cong were now burning the market. The Bankers ate early and were entering their newly expanded indoor bunker when their Vietnamese friend Ba arrived at the house bearing good news: a U.S. army helicopter had landed just around the corner.

"Quick!" she said, "Run and see if you can get a ride out. Things will be very hard for you if you stay. Even your neighbors are fleeing to spend the night in the Catholic church or wherever they can find safety."

John sprinted to the corner of the street; through his mind flashed the thought that he was now a running target! Betty hurriedly put shoes on the children, preparing them to escape to safety.

John turned the corner and saw a helicopter sitting just 100 yards from him. He ran. It was now only 50 feet away; their rescue was imminent! The helicopter rotors sliced through the air as the helicopter took off heading for safety, leaving John in the dust. Had they not seen him? John sprinted back home with the crushing news.

Ba returned, "Quick, there is another helicopter!" John was off again. But once again, the chopper took off and whirled away as he approached.

Ba had previously worked for the Bankers but now for the American officials who were being evacuated by helicopter

UNSTOPPABLE!

down the street. She ran down to those homes herself to check if the helicopters would be back.

She returned with disappointing news. There would be no more helicopters; all the Americans living there had been evacuated. Later Betty wrote home:

> It was obvious by now that no one was able to come get us. Our help would come from a far more dependable, higher source—the Lord Himself. What a wonderful comfort it was to realize that.

John and Betty and the children all climbed into their homemade bunker for another night. The children lay side by side on the mattresses under the tables. John and Betty sat or reclined at the entrance.

Abruptly a car drove into the yard. An unexpected voice called out, "Anyone home?" It was missionary colleague Lois Lee.

John opened the door. He and Betty expected to hear good news of rescue. Instead, the Lees, along with their language helpers, had come because they too were escaping from trouble. Their house was near the airport, which was even closer to the fighting. The noise the Bankers had heard so loudly was the gunships flying right over their house on the way to fight the enemy attacking the airport.

Lois with Roglai children

The Lees had spent Monday night in their bunker with their Roglai helper and her two children. On Tuesday they saw the Vietnamese people near them pack their clothes and leave. They also saw the American bombers striving to stop the NVA troops.

Late in the day they fled to the Bankers' home in search of a safer hideout. "You are two blocks further away from the battle than we were," Ernie said.

Happy to have company, the Bankers found spaces for each one in other protected areas of the house. Some were in the hall on mattresses and others behind the sofa in the living room. They all settled down to spend another long, restless night.

It took a long time for the children to get to sleep. The heat was miserably oppressive; "personal space" was out of the question. Every time one person moved it disturbed someone else. Finally, every one of the children slept from exhaustion.

But for Betty, it was the longest, noisiest, most nerve-wracking night she had ever experienced. The endless hours echoed with the sounds of American gunships flying overhead and shooting nearby.

As she sat waiting for the night to end, Betty thought, *What a crazy situation to be in with five small children, two of them not even our own.*

But the Lord encouraged Betty once again, as He had the night before. The words from Psalm 103:13 spoke to her heart, "As a Father has compassion on his children, so the Lord has compassion on those who fear Him."

Finally, Wednesday morning daylight pushed back the darkness and the noise of battle faded away. Many things

UNSTOPPABLE!

demanded attention, such as cooking enough food to feed the fourteen people now staying in the house.

John's Bahnar co-translator, He'i, left to check on the situation in the city and determine whether it was safe for the Lees to go home. They certainly were ready to get back to less cramped quarters.

He'i was able to go through the streets without catching anyone's attention. He found the Lees' house in order, along with the Roglai boys who had spent the night there.

He also checked on the other missionary family in town, the Coopers; they too were fine. The Coopers had finished making a bunker just before the fighting started on Monday night. They had spent two nights in that bunker hoping that in the morning the VC would disappear, as they usually did—but not this time.

He'i tried to reach the linguistic center where the other missionary families were. Unable to pass through the streets heading that direction, he turned around and headed back to the Bankers' home.

Wednesday night fourteen people sat down to dinner: the Bankers and their "extra" children, the Lees, and language helpers. As they were finishing, the rumbling of a motorbike sounded in the driveway.

This time it was Jim Cooper bringing a message from Doctor Pat Smith, who in the past had treated the missionaries and their children. Pat had bravely driven through the embattled city from the American Military Compound (MAC-V) on her way back to the Catholic hospital where she worked. She stopped on her way to relay a message from the American military to the missionaries. "The military is concerned about your three families [Coopers, Lees, Bankers]. They are urging you to make every effort to reach MAC-V where you can be safe. Your fellow workers from the linguistic center near MAC-V are all safely there now, but are concerned for you."

"However, it is now impossible for the military to come rescue your families by helicopter or armored personnel carriers because the area of Kontum is surrounded by 1,000 Viet Cong in plain clothes plus many more of the North Vietnamese Army. It is safer if you stay put than for the military to come get you."

She finished with the words, "I'm going back to my patients at the hospital."

With this news Bankers, Lees, and Coopers decided they needed to try to get to the military base. The Bankers grabbed their packed suitcases, and along with the children piled into the Volkswagen van. The seats were removed. Everyone sat on the floor; only the driver's head could be seen. The Lees did the same in their Land Rover.

UNSTOPPABLE!

Jim Cooper had taken off on his motorcycle to get his family ready to be picked up by the entourage. Just as Bankers and Lees started the vehicles, ready to head out, Jim zoomed back into the yard with a warning, "Wait, not that way! We need to take a different road. My neighbor just told me three Viet Cong are behind a pile of rocks on the road which I just took—the one I previously told you to take!"

Taking an alternate route as quickly as possible, the Lees went home to drop off their language helpers. By the time they met back up with the rest at Coopers' house, the whole Cooper family was ready. They piled in the Volkswagen alongside the Lees and Bankers, six adults and ten children all told.

With only the driver visible, they headed for the MAC-V compound on the other side of Kontum. Weaving through back streets, avoiding government buildings and the main market, the missionaries still had to pass through part of the town already in Communist control.

It was a very dangerous drive! Enemy soldiers were spread throughout the city—yet, miraculously, no one along the way seemed to notice them.

Holding their breath, they were just pulling up to the MAC-V compound gate, when suddenly—BOOM!! A loud explosion detonated in the field across from the compound! Someone had thrown a grenade at the gate and missed.

An alarm sounded and everyone at MAC-V ran for cover. The Bankers waited outside the gate in the van with their friends for what seemed an eternity. Uniformed personnel scurried here and there to check the situation, returning fire where the grenade had exploded.

When everything calmed down, the gate swung open. With relief the three families drove onto the base.

The armed soldiers, and even the barbed wire fences, brought a sense of relief and security after the past few days. It was so good to see their fellow workers who had been evacuated by helicopter the evening before.

As they jumped out of the vehicle in front of the soldiers and other missionaries, one GI commented in amazement, "You people lead charmed lives!"

The GIs, too busy to spend much time in their quarters, gave up their rooms for the missionary families. The Bankers took them up on their offer.

Earlier that same Wednesday the commander had called the missionaries already at the base and informed them, "The North Vietnamese Army (NVA) used your buildings as a staging center last night. You got out just in time. They've left now, but we will have to destroy the buildings to keep them from coming back there again tonight."

Approximately 6,500 North Vietnamese soldiers were now moving about in the surrounding area. From the linguistic center the NVA soldiers were in the perfect location to attack the Special Forces compound located just over a half mile away.

Ken Gregerson and the other missionaries quickly replied, "Go ahead and destroy the linguistic center. We will be sad to lose it, but saving lives is what matters now."

UNSTOPPABLE!

Dave Blood and a few other missionaries accompanied a demolition squad to the linguistic center. They gathered up typewriters, important books, language materials and some household equipment.

Dave was the last missionary to leave. He was pushing a refrigerator onto the back of a truck when the eerie silence was broken by the raucous chatter of a 50-calibre machine gun. Dave ran and jumped into a bunker close by.

The key in the truck's ignition turned, its engine now bursting to life as the driver quickly tried to escape the fusillade of bullets.

What was Dave to do? If he stayed, surely he would be shot or captured by the Viet Cong. If he ran for the truck, he could be cut down before he ever reached it. Dave made an instant decision and ran for his life. Sprinting as fast as he could, he jumped into the back of the truck.

The fleeing truck rocked around a corner, toppling the refrigerator sideways on top of Dave—and saving his life as the 50-cal machine gun again erupted. Two Montagnard government soldiers accompanying the truck fell victims to the deadly spray. Only the missionaries and the driver made it back to the base alive.

UNSTOPPABLE!

The North Vietnamese Army then took over the linguistic center. They used it as a staging area to attack the Special Forces and MAC-V bases. The linguistic center became a battlefield that resulted in its total destruction over the next two days (see photo below).

Wednesday evening the missionaries at Camp MAC-V all headed to dinner at the mess hall and waited outside for dinner to be served. A helicopter pilot flying overhead saw the Viet Cong drop a mortar round into the tube and radioed MAC-V. The alarm sounded. Everyone ran for the bunkers, finding protection before the mortar landed.

Ages went by, it seemed, before everything settled down. Then the Bankers and others were moved to a smaller bunker assigned to them for the night. They were given an air mattress, blanket, container of water and an empty can. Soon the chaplain brought C-rations for supper. The children thought everything was great fun.

Eventually settling down for the night, the girls lay on the air mattress and the boys on the blanket with their heads on the air mattress. Amazingly, the children slept soundly all night.

But John and Betty slept very little. The night before had seemed awfully noisy but it didn't compare at all to this night. This time they were in the middle of the fight, as the base itself was under attack.

To Carolyn Miller's mind came God's promise to the Apostle Paul during the storm at sea. "Do not be afraid Paul...God has graciously given you the lives of all who sail with you."[7]

Carolyn felt God impressing upon her heart that He would save the lives of everyone at MAC-V as long as the missionaries were there. She prayed for the American soldiers battling through the night as well as for her own family and colleagues.

The fierce fighting Wednesday night repeated the terrible onslaught of the night before. The suicidal waves of attacks came again and again. In the middle of the night the siren sounded, the Viet Cong had breached the fence on one side.

By morning the VC retreated over the dead bodies of many of their own; an uneasy peace ensued. American soldiers counted 960 North Vietnamese dead; 90 were bodies of soldiers trying to get through the barbed wire fence. Fewer than a dozen South Vietnamese soldiers lay dead.

---

[7] Acts 27:24

UNSTOPPABLE!

Although outnumbered ten to one, not a single soldier on the army base had been hit by enemy fire. One GI said, "It's a miracle that we are still alive!"

"It's incredible!" exclaimed the army chaplain to the missionaries, "I have never been in a worse situation. At times the attackers were literally coming over the fence, and it seemed we couldn't hold them off any longer. Yet in all that fighting the only injury we sustained was when one man sprained his ankle jumping into a trench."

"Well, Chaplain," said Carolyn, "we were praying."

He looked at her, amused, "Maybe we ought to invite you over every time we get attacked."

What a relief to have the enemy disappear with the darkness. The missionaries were able to move back into the soldiers' rooms for the day. The cooks prepared the meals in the mess hall kitchen. John and the other dads brought food to the rooms for their families; the soldiers did not want everybody congregating together in the open.

Since the soldiers had been fighting all night and needed some rest during the day, the missionary men helped by washing dishes and doing other chores. They sang a hymn as they went about their work. John Banker and Jim Cooper cleaned the latrines.

When the Bankers had first arrived at MAC-V, the chaplain told them they would probably be evacuated right away. But after the long night in the bunker, plans changed; more likely it would probably take five or six days of fighting before it would be safe enough to evacuate.

UNSTOPPABLE!

The Bankers and the others prepared themselves for more nights like the last one. Suddenly a soldier appeared and announced that the missionaries needed to be ready to be evacuated to Nha Trang in 15 minutes. The Bankers ran to the room and stuffed their belongings back in their suitcases.

The missionaries, 18 adults and 20 children in number, along with some of the locals who helped them with translation, gathered in the appointed place. The suitcases were all loaded onto one truck and the people onto the back of a second truck.

Pointing to all the baggage, Pat Cohen announced, "You can't get all that on the plane. And there's more stuff at the house across town. I'll stay here and keep an eye out for looters until you guys come back."

The officers tried to convince Pat to change his mind but they were unsuccessful. Finally, one of the officers said, "Let him stick around. We may need his prayers."

Armed jeeps surrounded the missionaries for protection as they headed for the airport. They were saddened to see parts of the city destroyed.

Arriving without incident at the airport, they awaited the Air America C-47 to take them to safety. They had been told there might not be room for everyone on the flight. Each woman wondered whether her husband might be left behind. What a relief when the flight arrived and room was found for everyone; many in the group were small children.

An hour and 15 minutes later they arrived in Nha Trang, where they were taken by bus to Camp McDermott, the

UNSTOPPABLE!

American Army base. It was February 1st. Two of the missionaries celebrated their birthdays that day: Doris Blood and Ruthie Philipps.

That night back in Kontum, the North Vietnamese Army (NVA) attacked the MAC-V military post again, fighting all through the night until 7am. The opposition was so fierce that the Americans had to call in fire from the helicopter gunships on their own positions. In the morning they found some 60 dead bodies of the NVA within the base perimeter and 260 dead bodies outside.[8]

Pat Cohen had stayed behind to look after the literacy and translation workers from the minority languages involved in the recent workshops with the missionaries. When Pat's immediate area came under rocket attack, the Bahnar translator under Pat's care trembled in fear as he ducked under Pat to shield himself from the in-coming shells.

Fighting and destruction occurred all across South Viet Nam during the Chinese New Year celebrations. By Tuesday noon half of Pleiku was destroyed. The Alliance missionaries who worked with John and Betty were rescued by a contingent of U.S. Army soldiers and taken to a base four miles outside of the city and then flown to Nha Trang.

A battle raged right next to the house where four volunteers with the Viet Nam Christian Service (VNCS) were hiding. There was no way out; the situation was desperate.

---

[8] This information comes primarily from personal communication with those who experienced these events.

UNSTOPPABLE!

Suddenly, a group of U.S. soldiers, some of them wounded, broke into the house. A wounded Special Forces captain shouted at them, "Quick, follow us out through the back way. The VC are all over the street in front." Despite his own injuries, the captain led them outside and to the other side of the block. They were loaded into military ambulances along with wounded soldiers and taken to the airport.

They were evacuated to safety, along with four other VNCS workers. But the Special Forces captain, critically wounded, remained in Pleiku. Beside his bed sat a nurse, Rebecca Gould, one of the VNCS workers whom he had helped rescue.

Rebecca raised her head from prayer and said to him, "I will stick with you. You are going to be all right."

Three months later they were married.

Ban Me Thuot (Tet 1968)

Hank Blood, John and Betty's colleague and translator for one of the other ethnic minority people groups, felt a growing burden to disciple them. A young man named Talla had heard the gospel from Rade pastors but struggled to really understand because the explanation was not in his mother tongue. Every day as Talla taught Hank to speak his language, Hank taught Talla a few verses and explained them. Hank also taught him to pray.

Talla later said:

At first, I didn't understand what Hank taught me. But after I had been with him some months, I found that my heart was thirsting very much for the Word of God, and I was moved to receive Jesus Christ as my Savior. He taught me much about grace and love, and he counted me as his own son.

Around this time Hank wrote to his fellow missionaries:

Let's all remember that this is not the end of the story. This is a time to trust the Lord and to do what we can. As we pray, the Lord is able to open doors. I believe there will yet come a time in this country when those in our group who already have some knowledge of the tribal languages will have their great day of opportunity...for others of us this day has not yet arrived....Lead on, O King Eternal, till sin's fierce wars shall cease—till holiness shall whisper the sweet Amen of peace.

The Hank Blood family lived in Ban Me Thuot close to the grounds of the Rade Bible School. Highway 14 ran through the Alliance compound separating the Rade Bible School from the Alliance houses, clinic and church. It went on to the headquarters of the Darlac Provincial offices and the business part of town, making it a very busy road, and also a dangerous one in wartime.

The U.S. military base was about four miles away, as was the U.S. 155th Helicopter base. The South Vietnamese Army base was situated just behind the compound. Equipped with tanks and heavy artillery, it guarded those coming toward Ban Me Thuot from the south.

The missionaries remained neutral, stockpiling no arms or even setting up barbed wire fences to protect themselves. They realized that even if they weren't the target of enemy attack, they could easily get caught in the middle. But they entrusted their lives to God's providence.

One of these missionaries was Ruth Thompson. She had previously written to her children in college saying, "Didn't you know we are immortal until our work is done?"

Another missionary, Betty Olsen, answered a question put forth by Hal Boyles. He had asked, "Don't you feel uneasy at being in a war zone?"

She said, "I have no fear because I am in the will of God."

On Monday evening, the eve of Tet, the missionaries in Ban Me Thuot went to bed as usual with the normal sounds of celebration and firecrackers popping in their ears. But at 1am the sound became painfully loud.

Bob Zeimer sat up and said to his wife. "Listen! That's artillery and small arms fire. Nothing we can do about it but pray and hope they won't hit us."

The Thompsons, Griswolds, and Bloods also heard the noise. The Hank Bloods moved to their landlord's bunker with their blankets and flashlights.

The missionaries were in a very precarious spot, surrounded on one side by the Viet Cong and the other by the South Vietnamese soldiers. The U.S. Military base was desperately fighting its own continuous ground assault. The American helicopter base in the area also came under intense enemy fire; all but two of their helicopters were destroyed.

An explosion rocked the home of C&MA's Carolyn Griswold and her father, killing Carolyn's father. Other C&MA

missionaries dug seriously-wounded Carolyn out of her collapsed home. Later she died from her injuries.

Through the next couple of days, fighting closed in on them. Avoiding discovery, the C&MA missionaries left their houses and found shelter in a garbage pit turned bunker.

Wycliffe's Hank Blood and family were found by Communist soldiers in their home. They were all held captive overnight along with many of the local people. During that time Hank led one of the other captives to the Lord.

Hank along with C&MA's Betty Olsen and U.S. AID's Mike Benge were taken off into captivity in the jungle never to be seen by his family again. Hank said goodbye to his wife with the words, "Tell the others that the Lord has done something special for me and I'm ready."

Later Hank's language helper, Talla, expressed his grief:
Oh Mr. Henry Blood!
I am very sad that you have gone away.
Oh Sir: We no longer meet face to face.
Oh Sir: My heart still remembers you.
Oh Sir: I bless your soul, wishing it continual happiness in the Lord.
Right now, I greet you with a sorrowful heart.
Lonesome for you, who are reclining in the name of the Lord.
Hoping that your spirit's having peace and happiness because I still retain what you taught me.
The Lord will take care of your body as it is lost in the jungle.
May the Holy Spirit comfort your wife and children while they are still in this world. Amen.[9]

---

[9] Taken from the Viet Nam Praise and Prayer Bulletin, May 1973.

UNSTOPPABLE!

Hank's wife, Vange, and their three children, along with Marie Ziemer, though wounded, made it back to safety.

Armed soldiers discovered the sheltering C&MA missionaries in the pit and gunned them down. Edward and Ruth Thompson, Bob Ziemer and Ruth Wilting, [whose fiancé had been captured six years previously,] died instantly.

Twelve days after the deaths of the C&MA missionaries, Gene Evans and Richard Phillips arrived at Ban Me Thuot. Soldiers accompanied them as they went to recover the bodies of those who had given their lives for the Gospel. They found them lying face down with Ed Thompson shielding his wife, Ruth.

Dick stooped to pick up a piece of paper. It appeared to have been left from a hymn book. Cleaning off the paper, he read the first stanza:

> Anywhere with Jesus I can safely go.
> Anywhere He leads me in this world below.
> Anywhere without Him dearest joys would fade.
> Anywhere with Jesus I am not afraid.[10]

Changes (1968)

The missionary families who evacuated from Camp MAC-V, bearing only the clothes quickly tossed into their suitcases, were taken to Camp McDermott in Nha Trang. At the military base they received gifts of clothing as well as oranges, apples, and candy. The Bankers' furniture that had been at the

---

[10] The accounts from Tet '68 in Pleiku and Ban Me Thuot are taken from the book *By Life or By Death* (Hefley, 1969).

linguistic center in Kontum, along with their store of Bahnar primers and teaching materials were all destroyed. But their possessions at the Children's Home and school miraculously survived.

The missionaries remained at Camp McDermott for 18 days. They shared a round barracks and enjoyed eating the special food served in the mess hall. The parents were thankful for the sense of security. The children played as if it was life as usual, except for one girl who had her stomach pumped after eating rat poison.

The ocean right in front of the base was beautiful. The children splashed in the water and jumped the rolling waves with delight.

The adults found opportunities to share their faith. John and others spoke at various chapels, including a Signal Battalion chapel.

Soon after arriving in Nha Trang a letter arrived for the Bankers. "What was happening to you the week of January 29?" It read, "God woke me in the night and put a heavy burden on my heart for you. I gathered several women together and we prayed." The letter was from Grammy Payton[11], a faithful prayer warrior from the Tabers' church in Ellington, CT.

---

[11] Grammy Payton is Mark Taber's maternal grandmother.

UNSTOPPABLE!

Betty's mother also wrote, saying God had awakened her in the night. She felt Betty was in trouble and so she cried out to God on her daughter's behalf.

What comfort those letters brought to their hearts, reminding them of God's love and confirming His hand of protection over their lives. The timing of their prayers coincided exactly with when they were under enemy gunfire.

After nearly three weeks in the camp, the colonel told the missionaries it was now safe to leave Camp McDermott. They were given a 12-room house in Nha Trang with sufficient space for four or five families.

The Viet Cong had suffered heavy losses back in Kontum. The colonel from MAC-V also communicated that it was now safe enough for the missionaries to return if they wished.

Despite these assurances, most of the wives and families from the various missions serving in Viet Nam were asked to leave temporarily—not by the U.S. Embassy but by the sending agencies. Even the wives and children of the Bible translators were instructed to leave for a time unless they could give some good reason for their decision to stay. And having departed Viet Nam, any decision to return must first be cleared with their director.

John wrote home to his parents at this time:

> We do think about you all the time and know that we have caused you great concern. This in turn causes us great concern, too, for we love you very much. Pray that we know and do the Lord's will.

UNSTOPPABLE!

John and Betty decided to leave and spend some time in the Philippines. While there, they hoped to enroll Tommy and Kathy into school, and await the birth of Nancy, their fourth child. They still had much to work on during the time away. The textbooks for the Bahnar multi-education program needed to be typed in preparation for printing.

On their way out of the country, they stopped in Saigon for a few days. John wrote home:

> We are glad to have a room all to ourselves now. In Nha Trang we slept in the same room with two or three other families. Some of our people are still there at the base in Nha Trang. The food supply here in Saigon is fine. We had ice cream today.

Upon arriving in the Philippines, John wrote:

> We thank the Lord for a safe trip to Manila two days ago. We came on a Pan Am jet. We were taken to the missionary group house where we will be staying for a few days. Then we plan to go to the missionary base at Bagabag on this same island. We would like to go to the missionary base called Nasuli but it is too crowded now. This house has much more space for playing outside than the Saigon house or the army camp we were at. They have swings and a teeter-totter here, too.

> Didn't you receive a telephone call the first week in February from Santa Ana saying that we were all right? Hank Blood has been seen by Rade tribespeople who were at the prison camp he was, but then they were released. They said he seemed to be okay.

> Everything is very quiet and peaceful here [Bagabag, Philippines]. People here at the base don't even lock their

doors at night. They usually turn off the lights [electricity] about 9:00pm so we go to bed early. The kids enjoy all the space to run and play."

John, never one to stay idle, edited the Bahnar draft of the Book of Acts that he and He'i had recently finished while still in Viet Nam. He endeavored to improve the translation in passages of scripture he felt were not yet quite right. To really fix the translation properly he needed Bahnar speakers. But when would this be possible?

In mid-April 1968 John left Betty and their three children in Bagabag, Philippines where it was safe and returned to Viet Nam. He made his way back to the towns of Nha Trang, Kontum and Pleiku. In Kontum he picked up some of their possessions to bring back, including some of the kids' toys.

While still in Pleiku, John spent significant time with Om, who was growing in his faith. Sometimes Om held Sunday evening services in his home. He also worked for the Viet Nam Christian Service as an interpreter. Regularly Om went to the village with two VNCS missionaries, passing out soup, helping treat the sick, and improving the villagers' health. At times he even cut hair for the people.

John was gone for six long weeks. He missed Betty and the children dearly. He wrote home to his parents, "I think I'm getting to know some of the loneliness you have had when all your children are away. What makes it doubly hard is not having Betty here either."

While John was away, Betty wrote to John's parents:

UNSTOPPABLE!

Tommy and Mary Alice are here beside the table eating a tropical fruit that is similar to a grapefruit but not so juicy and sour.

Tommy doesn't have any boyfriends here and there is no one Mary Alice's age so they stick pretty close together and really seem to enjoy each other. Mary Alice likes airplanes about as well as Tommy. Kathy is out with her friends. There are 7 girls here now so Kathy has a wonderful time. She really enjoys her friends.

A few days ago we found a snake curled up in a corner under Tommy's bed. It was a fairly harmless one but gave me a start when I pulled the bed out to wash the floor! Some of the Filipino girls here killed it.

For a number of weeks John sought to get the paperwork needed to bring He'i and family to the Philippines so they could again work together, but he never succeeded. In the end, He'i and his family returned to Pleiku. John went back to the Philippines without his much-loved Bahnar co-translator.

Back in Bagabag, John set to work typing up another textbook for the Bahnar multi-lingual education project. It was the translation of a Vietnamese primer to be used for the second year of the Bahnar children's schooling, enabling them to understand what they were learning to read in Vietnamese.

John's varied projects included preparing for the translation of additional books, writing up the findings regarding Bahnar culture, and typing a concordance (a type of dictionary that gives the occurrences of words in their contexts).

UNSTOPPABLE!

July 15, 1968 was the first day of school for Tommy and Kathy at Nancy Knoblock School located on the linguistic center in Nasuli, Philippines. Their residence during the school term would be the Children's Home called Happy Holler, shared with an additional 16 schoolmates.

Tommy moved into Happy Holler right away. But, sick with bronchitis, Kathy remained with her parents another night. She cried because she so wanted to be in the Children's Home just like her brother.

The next day John Miller took her to the missionary hospital at Malaybalay, 12 miles away. John and Betty postponed their trip back to Manila for several days. It was very difficult for John and Betty to leave Kathy. *What would happen if she got another one of her infections?* They had hoped to have a place to stay in Nasuli and perhaps help out there so as to be near the children. When that didn't work out, they made plans to go back to Manila, where John would be an administrative assistant to the director of the translation work in the Philippines while they waited for their baby to be born.

When their parents did leave for Manila, Tom and Kathy shed no tears. But little Mary Alice did; she would miss her brother and sister.

UNSTOPPABLE!

Later in September the Bankers welcomed little Nancy Ann into the family. John wrote home:

> She looks a lot like Kathy did when she was first born....The pediatrician checked the baby and said everything is okay. Betty is doing well, too. So we thank the Lord for these things.

The Return (1968-69)

On November 15, 1968 John wrote home to his parents:

> We are getting anxious to get back to the work the Lord has called us to in Viet Nam. From all reports, things are much better there now. We would not plan to live in Kontum or Pleiku now, but would live in Nha Trang which seems to be one of the most secure places in Viet Nam.
>
> The hardest thing about going back is knowing the worry it might cause you. This is one of the reasons we haven't gone back before now. But now it seems that it's God's time for us to go back and things are better there now security-wise.

The next day John received a letter from Dick Watson, their director in Viet Nam:

> The situation here has steadily improved since Tet until now. I feel that it is better than it has been for the past couple of years. There is a new morale and determination among the Vietnamese and both the U.S. and V.N. military.
>
> A town like Kontum, for instance, probably has at least four times more troops and better defenses than at Tet and furthermore, the civilians have formed community

guards so that every area of town is patrolled by the best men in the neighborhood and communication is maintained throughout the town.

Jim Cooper's neighbors have assured him that since they have opportunity to participate now, they can guarantee that the type of thing that happened at Tet can never happen again.

Both the Coopers and Gregersons feel relaxed and much at home again in Kontum and I believe that you would too.

Nha Trang, of course, is even quieter. In addition to the usual urgency for Bahnar work, Franklin Irwin and Rev. Men have both spoken to us requesting our special help in preparation of tribal materials, particularly in Bahnar and Jarai for their Evangelism-in-Depth program to begin soon. Gail Fleming is anxious to see you again about this.

Two weeks later John, Betty, Mary Alice, and baby Nancy returned to Viet Nam. Tommy and Kathy remained in school in the Philippines for another month.

Back in Nha Trang, the Bankers again connected with Hiu, the Bahnar teacher who had helped translate the liturgy. Hiu joined them for Thanksgiving dinner before returning to Kontum. John was so happy to be back with the Bahnar people once again.

John traveled to Kontum to bring what was left of their belongings to Nha Trang to set up house there. He also went to Pleiku to see if He'i could come continue with the translation. He'i was at a camp out from An Khe so John tried to contact him by letter. *And if Hei cannot come to help, perhaps the Lord has someone else who might work with me,* John thought.

Almost as soon as John arrived back in Nha Trang, he departed to Saigon to get Tommy and Kathy, who were coming from the Philippines for Christmas. John wrote home:

> It will be so good to see them again and then to be all together again in Nha Trang. I plan to take our artificial Christmas tree back to Nha Trang. We thank the Lord that we have lost very few of the things that we left in the house here in Kontum.

Then later:

> Our Christmas vacation is a little different than yours—we have been going to the beach every day. The waves are pretty high so the kids just play in the breakers as they splash upon the beach. They think it is great fun though.
>
> I bought a 12-pound turkey at the commissary in Saigon so we will have that at Christmas. There will be the Fippingers and Eugenia Johnston and us plus any guests that may be invited.
>
> We ended up including the Coopers, Gregersons, Pat Cohen, and Nancy Howlison who came in unexpectedly the day before Christmas. Someone remarked that our Christmas dinner was the best one served in Viet Nam. It was a really good one.
>
> Everything seems very peaceful here. We gave a soldier a ride the other day. He has been working in the Danang area. He said that the people down here in Nha Trang don't even know there is a war going on, somewhat different from where he is.

UNSTOPPABLE!

In mid-January 1969 John returned to Pleiku to see if He'i would be willing to come continue the translation in Nha Trang. He was!

While in Pleiku, John and He'i went to speak at a service at the C&MA leprosarium. Among those being treated for this disfiguring disease were a number of Bahnar who had been living in the jungle until recently being brought to the leprosarium. John felt great pity in his heart when he looked at them. He'i asked if anyone wanted to believe in Jesus. Three people came forward and prayed to accept Christ.

When John and He'i returned to Nha Trang, they met a Christian Bahnar man who was studying to be a lab technician. He was training to work at the leprosarium at Pleiku.

In Nha Trang, John and He'i prepared for the upcoming translation workshop. They translated hymns and continued the second draft of the Book of Acts to be checked by a colleague. In late January six and one-half chapters of Acts along with a few chapters of Acts in the Chrau language were checked. Then John and He'i began work on 1 Timothy.

Betty's hands were always full helping out in many ways. She worked on a new set of educational primers to replace those destroyed in the battle during the Tet offensive. In Pleiku province alone, they were asking for 1500 copies.

John wrote home regularly to his parents about their grandchildren:

> The ocean is very beautiful here. We don't get out there very often now that the kids have gone back to school.
>
> Three more months until Tommy and Kathy come home for their summer vacation. They will have about a two-and-a-half-month vacation. Mary Alice has fun with quite a few kids here. They are going to her Sunday School now and she's all excited about it. It wasn't too long ago when she wouldn't go to Sunday School alone. Nancy started crawling last week. However, she hasn't learned how to crawl the regular way yet.

In February 1969, a year after the previous year's battle during the Tet celebration, John wrote home: "We are thankful that we had a quiet Tet this year, very few firecrackers even. I guess they were outlawed."

By the end of February, the consultant check of Bahnar Acts was completed. John and He'i next worked on 1 Thessalonians. Due to security issues, John didn't know when or how he would be able to get to the village to do the necessary comprehension checks with Bahnar speakers.

In mid-March he wrote home:

> Everything is very peaceful here. We did not have a major attack here like the map in the magazine seemed to indicate. The only thing we had here in 1969 was a mortaring of the military outside of town and one terrorist incident. It is very quiet at night.

UNSTOPPABLE!

Then in early April he wrote home again:

We thank the Lord for all the translation we were able to get done. I'll list the books again: Acts checked; 1&2 Thessalonians, 1&2 Timothy, Titus and Philemon translated and checked.

We sang at the Easter sunrise service this morning on the beach. There was a good crowd of servicemen there. The Vietnamese Bible school choir sang and they did very well. There must have been about 20 missionaries in the missionary choir.

On Friday I will go to Saigon to get Tommy and Kathy. They will come on Saturday with Lois Lee. The next day we will plan to fly back here. Won't that be a happy day.

Mary Alice was running upstairs today and fell down and bumped her chin and it was cut open. We took her to the Eighth Army Field Hospital here in Nha Trang, and had her stitched up. It took four stitches. She was a very good girl though; she cried just a little.

John and He'i began translating a few Bible stories that the Bible Society would later print in an attractive folder with colored pictures. Next John and He'i planned to translate the Gospel of John.

Tom and Kathy returned from the Philippines for their holidays. The Bankers, along with their other colleagues and families, enjoyed vacation time swimming and picnicking at the beautiful beaches. John and Betty took the children to the Air Force chapel on Sunday so the children could understand the services.

In May 1969 John wrote home:

He'i and I have been working on both John and Matthew. He has been doing a first draft of parts of Matthew and then I come along and correct it and help him with difficult verses. I am doing a first draft on John and he is correcting that.

We praise the Lord that He'i seems to be quite happy here.

It is true that we have been lacking in support, not getting as much as is set by Wycliffe for its full support figure. However, we have not been lacking in any way here, we have plenty. Well, we have to go wash the diapers, so I better quit.

In June He'i returned to Pleiku to spend time with his family. While he was gone John continued on with the anthropology paper he had started on Bahnar traditional religion at the workshop in Kontum just before the big battle of Tet had begun the previous year.

Tommy and Kathy's vacation was quickly passing. Soon they would return to school in the Philippines. To maximize their time together, the Banker family enjoyed many fun activities. They managed to get to the beach four times in a week while also accomplishing a lot of work at home, too. Little Nancy was beginning to stand by herself. Six-year-old Kathy sometimes took care of her.

UNSTOPPABLE!

In mid-1969 John wrote home:

A funny thing happened the other day. Ken Hutchinson and I went to an American mess hall to get some food. After the serviceman finished giving us the food he said, "And now I want to touch your car," which he did and didn't say any more. I suppose he hadn't seen a civilian car for a long time and he liked the looks of it. It was the VW Microbus. We are thinking about moving to Pleiku for a few months, until the kids come home for Christmas or maybe until they go back in early January. After that we will come back here for a translation workshop.

Pleiku has been quiet for several months now. There are 20-30,000 troops in the immediate area of Pleiku, Americans, that is. The Flemings are moving back soon too and we plan to live next to them on the C&MA compound. We believe that this is the Lord's leading at this time.

In August 1969, after Tommy and Kathy returned to school in the Philippines, John went to Pleiku to prepare a house for the family to move into. One of the homes which the C&MA missionaries had bought from the French many years previously was made available to them. A lot of cleaning was needed, as no one had lived there since the time of the Tet hostilities. This would be the first time in a year and a half that the Bankers had lived in a house all by themselves.

Their neighbors on both sides were C&MA missionaries and both had a television. This was because the 42nd Division base camp not too far way operated a TV station. One afternoon the head chaplain of the 16th Division came to visit the Flemings. The chaplain wanted to interview some of the missionaries on a TV program he produced at the 42th Division.

Back at school in the Philippines, the fevers and urinary tract infections that Kathy had struggled with regularly from early childhood continued. The surgery Kathy had undergone as a very young girl to rectify the problem seemed to bring no improvement. Her fevers began to soar again.

One night, although Kathy's parents were far away in Viet Nam, God answered the prayers of her godly dorm mother, Sadie Seeker. Sadie had seen the Lord heal many people in amazing ways during her long years of serving the Lord across the Philippines; in fact, the Lord had healed her from heart attacks.

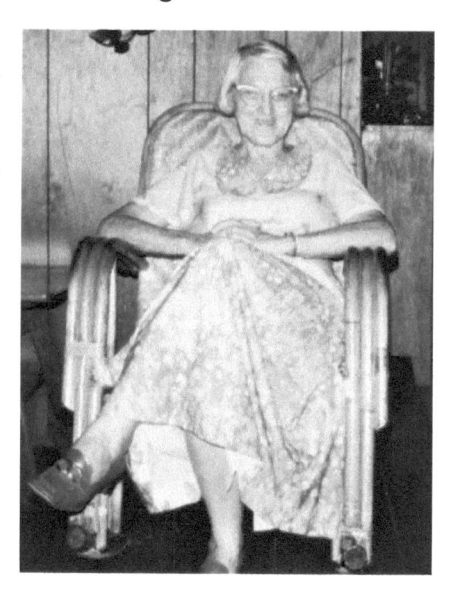

When sickness struck Kathy again, Sadie called a couple of her friends who knew how to pray. They called out to God on Kathy's behalf. From that day the sickness that had plagued her for the first six years of her life never bothered her again.

Kathy loved to listen to "Aunt" Sadie read stories about Jesus and His love. She began to fall in love with this Jesus. Because of "Aunt" Sadie's personal near-death experience, she had an ever-present longing for heaven and for seeing

UNSTOPPABLE!

her dear Savior. This love and intense desire, she communicated daily to the children.

Kathy, along with the many other children, learned to swim in the cold water of the spring-fed pool. They climbed in the abundant and varied tropical trees, hunting for fruit. Unripe fruit was claimed while still hanging on the tree as the kids carved their initials on it. When the fruit was ripe and juicy, they returned to enjoy it.

Their dorm father, "Uncle" Oscar had stuffed eels decorating the walls of his bedroom. The stories the children invented together to explain these snakes got wilder and wilder.

The same was true of the red ping pong paddle reportedly used for disciplinary purposes. Everyone was a little afraid of it. One of the children went to take a peek at it and insisted it was covered with nails!

UNSTOPPABLE!

Progress Made in a Season of Peace (1969-71)

Now back in Pleiku, the Bankers were able to attend worship services with the Bahnar people. This was a special blessing as obtaining permission to visit the villages had been difficult since the Bankers first started working among the Bahnar. It was wonderful to fellowship with them again!

Part of the translation process included checking if the translated scriptures were understandable to those who read or heard them. Being back in Pleiku enabled them to do this type of checking. Comprehension checks resulted in some helpful revisions. While He'i explained the scripture to the Bahnar man who assisted them, John listened intently. In this way he not only learned from the comments of the man, but also from He'i's explanations.

Once in a while, He'i himself did not understand the translated scriptures correctly. When this happened, it gave clues as to what words needed to be changed to make the text clear. Since much of the book could be understood by the checker, John and He'i felt more confident about the quality of their draft of Acts. This was the fifth time they had worked through Acts, either translating, checking, or revising.

What a tremendous blessing to see the Bahnar using the scriptures John and the translation team had worked together to translate! The Gospel of Mark they had translated first and officially published was now regularly used by the Bahnar pastor as he preached. The portions they had just recently finished, He'i used to teach about God in his own village, even though they had not yet been officially printed.

UNSTOPPABLE!

One night, He'i said, "Where is the Gospel of John that we have been translating this week? I want chapter nine. I have to preach in my village tomorrow."

He took the scripture portion to his village and preached the next morning. When he came back that afternoon, he said, "They really enjoyed the story of the blind man in John chapter nine!"

In mid-September He'i finished the draft of the Gospel of John. Then he looked over what John had done on the first two chapters of 1 John. It seemed to meet a need they had in the church, so he preached from it the next Sunday.

Not only were the scriptures impacting the lives of the Bahnar people, they were blessing and encouraging other people groups as well. John preached in Bahnar at a Jarai church, using 1-2 Thessalonians and 2 Timothy which he and He'i had recently translated. Then a Bahnar lay preacher interpreted John's message into the Jarai language for the people listening.

In October 1969 John wrote home:

UNSTOPPABLE!

We have had an interesting little boy on the compound this week....His father was off with the VC, his mother was killed and he himself was wounded in the arm. The Bahnar preacher decided to adopt him as his child.

He has been here this week to have surgery on his arm. He is staying with the two C&MA nurses.

He's a real cute little guy, maybe about 6 years old. He comes to play with Mary Alice sometimes. One of the soldiers gave him a cap with a captain's insignia and a lady's purse and he has been carrying those around.

Again in October 1969 John sent a letter to loved ones:

What a surprise we had this week. Gail Fleming asked me to go with him to the airport to pick up a load of candy that was coming in to be distributed to the tribal people [from World Relief Commission of the NAE].

There was so much candy in that shipment for the tribal people that we couldn't get it all in one load in Gail's Land Rover pickup. And it was real good type candy, too—chocolate covered mints, chocolate covered nuts and some other kinds. Yesterday we went to a village and had a service and they passed out some there.

UNSTOPPABLE!

One of the villages in which they distributed the sweets was filled with many refugees brought in earlier in the year from remote areas. Among them were eleven Bahnar and some Jarai as well, with little exposure to the Gospel. Two Bahnar preachers spoke at the service with close to 200 people listening.

He'i went to the village to help with the rice harvest and then on to Ban Me Thuot for an Evangelism-in-Depth conference. Afterward, John and He'i continued work on the revision of the Gospel of Mark. John also worked with Gail Fleming and several Bahnar speakers to prepare an attractive Christmas story booklet to use for the upcoming holiday celebrations.

In November John and Betty flew to Kontum from Pleiku to hold a workshop for the multilingual education project they had been asked to do by the government. However, they didn't make it to their destination the first day. Normally the 30-mile flight took 15-20 minutes. But because it was so windy, they ended up flying the opposite direction to Nha Trang, then flew the longer distance back the next day.

Their colleague Ernie Lee and his Rade assistant Yach conducted the program until the Bankers arrived. Fifty-two teachers were involved, seven from Pleiku. Betty taught them how to make visual aids, word wheels, wall charts, and arithmetic charts.

While John and Betty were in Kontum they stayed with their friends, the Coopers, and celebrated Thanksgiving together. It was also John and Betty's 10th wedding Anniversary.

The next day they hoped to return to Pleiku but waited over four hours at the airport only to find no plane was coming. The next day they waited three hours. When it became apparent that the flight would not come that day either, they were offered a ride back home on a helicopter. Upon arriving in Pleiku, one of the soldiers on the helicopter used his truck to take them right to their home.

On December 7, John wrote home:

> Last night I was on a TV program at the TV station here near Pleiku. The head chaplain at the 4th Division interviewed me about our work. Betty and the children watched on Fleming's TV. It was the first TV program I had ever been on. The station is on the top of a hill called Dragon Mountain a little way out of Pleiku.

> We all just went for a ride on the Honda to visit Om and his family. We also went by the place where we used to live here in Pleiku. Nancy likes to ride on the Honda, she was singing on the way home. And she put on a show while we were at their place. She is 15 months now.

For Christmas, Tommy and Kathy returned home from school in the Philippines for several weeks. Pleiku, with its cooler weather, red dirt, poinsettias, and special Christmas celebrations in the village was a wonderful place to be at for Christmas! The children's two-week vacation passed too quickly and they headed back to school in the Philippines once again.

UNSTOPPABLE!

In February 1970, two years after the adventures leading up to their evacuation, the Bankers celebrated a very quiet Tet—one of the quietest they had ever experienced. Firecrackers had been outlawed for the Vietnamese three-day holiday.

After Tet, John helped the young Bahnar men working with him to get some plywood at the Army warehouse. The wood was being cleaned out because the unit was moving to Cam Ranh Bay. What a blessing to be able to use what the military was leaving behind to aid those involved in the translation work in their time of need.

Then came the day when the Bankers traveled from Pleiku to Nha Trang with the books of scripture they had been working on. A Bible translation workshop was about to begin during which John hoped to have the Gospel and Epistles of John checked by Dick Elkins, a translation consultant working in the Philippines. Once approved, these scriptures along with Mark's Gospel would be prepared for publication.

The Bankers were thankful He'i was willing to come down for the workshop. This was a sacrifice for He'i and his family; his baby and wife, who had recently become a Christian, could not make the trip.

The Vietnamese pastor who worked with the Jarai, South Viet Nam's largest tribe, attended the workshop too. He had a busy life, translating the Bible for the Jarai while also serving as director of a clinic and leprosarium in Pleiku.

The Bankers always enjoyed their time in Nha Trang, even though they lived in the crowded group house with many other missionaries. But they also enjoyed their time in Pleiku among the Bahnar people. There they had their own house, which was a real blessing.

Betty still had much work to do on the Bahnar primers and teacher's guide. She was busy working on the Vietnamese translation of the primers to be placed in the back of each of the primers. Some days she didn't seem to make much progress. Sometimes it was because of technical issues like waiting for carbon ribbons to come.

On other occasions important responsibilities took priority. A long flight of cement stairs stood at each end of the building they lived in and keeping little Nancy from falling down them was no small task. Sixteen-month-old Nancy had the energy of three her size. She chattered all the time though most of her words were unintelligible.

While in Nha Trang, the Bankers always made time to swim in the ocean. One of the beaches near the American Army base was called "The American Beach." American soldiers found rest there, eating hamburgers, hotdogs and drinking soda right on the beach. The missionary families happily joined in, while large waves rose high and fell crashing upon white shores. Unable to withstand the might of the waves, the children built sand castles and drank their first Dr. Peppers, while the forested mountains of Hon Tre island beckoned invitingly across the water.

The Bankers were thankful for the help they received from others. One day on their way home from the beach the Bankers got a flat tire. The vehicle had no spare tire or tools. Thankfully, they weren't too far from help. Some Christian Servicemen Center volunteers came to replace the tire and get them going on their way again.

The captain of one of the Military Police companies in Nha Trang was a fine Christian. He helped the missionaries finish cementing the grounds of their group house by providing premixed cement.

In December 1971 the Bankers returned to Pleiku. They were happy and encouraged to receive permission to spend Christmas in a Bahnar village. One of the speakers during the Christmas celebrations was a Rade pastor who had been captured with Hank Blood and later released, and now had a vital ministry.

Another speaker was Talla, who had been a language helper for Hank Blood and now was recognized as a key spiritual leader among his people. Talla shared how he had become a Christian because of the tremendous impact Hank had on his life. Through such testimonies of national believers, Hank's witness for the Lord was still bearing fruit.

By this time Hank, Betty Olsen, and Mike Benge had been in captivity for three years. No one really knew where they were or what was happening to them.

UNSTOPPABLE!

Yet Another Role to Serve the Lord
(late 1971-early 1972)

As 1971 drew to an end, the Bankers packed up their belongings in Pleiku and moved back to Nha Trang. This time they would be staying at the Children's Home located on the property of the Janie Makil Memorial School. The school was named after the little daughter of Gaspar Makil who, along with her father, had been killed by enemy fire in 1963.

For four months John and Betty were "dad" and "mom" to the school children whose parents were serving the Lord in other parts of Viet Nam. Their "family," including their own children, consisted of seventeen 1st through 5th graders. This was a very busy but rewarding time as they saw the Lord working in the lives of the children.

Mostly oblivious to the stresses of war, Tommy, Kathy, and Mary Alice enjoyed life with the other missionary children in Nha Trang. There was no end of adventures at the school located in the beautiful coastal city. What they studied in the classroom may have remained only a blur in their memories, but what they played would vividly live forever in their minds.

UNSTOPPABLE!

The school and Children's Home were situated on a sandy beach. Coconut trees swayed back and forth as the wind blew across the sparkling South China Sea. During the day the vivid blues of the ocean lay before them. At night a long line of fishermen's lights twinkled in the distance like a lighted highway.

When the children were not in class or doing homework, they were playing under the coconut trees, swimming and snorkeling in the ocean, or shell-hunting in crevasses in the coral. Huge rocks lay scattered for miles along the edge of the beach. The kids loved to scramble over these boulders, jumping from rock to rock.

UNSTOPPABLE!

They spent many hours playing games like *Red Rover* or *Kick the Can,* the second game always ending in arguments: "I caught you."

"No, you didn't!"

"Yes, I did!"

One of the children's favorite activities was to gather palm branches and "ride" them like horses as they acted out adventures of cowboys and Indians.

Sometimes they climbed up the guava tree searching for fruit, while the Coopers' pet monkey swung from the girls' hair like Tarzan swinging from vines. At times the monkey looked for imaginary lice in their hair and grabbed guavas out of their mouths.

The school itself was prime for adventure. On the property stood an old shed in which the children spent hours playing one type of make-believe game after another. Kathy loved to climb and managed to make it to the rooftop of every building on the property except the trailer.

Every weekend all the school children walked down the beach to the area where the best swimming could be found. They jumped waves for hours, or snorkeled right in front of the school property, catching angel fish or other brightly colored specimens of florescent aqua, black-and-white stripes, and other hues for their home-made aquarium.

Unfortunately, the kids weren't as good at keeping fish alive as at catching them, so they regularly had to capture a new stash from the sea to restock the aquarium. That was, until "Uncle" Jim Cooper built a real aquarium. Jim caught the bat fish which was dubbed "Leif Erickson." Leif managed to grow from a tiny leaf-looking creature to great size during his stay. He could be seen floating around regally in his spacious home.

Dogs and cats were among the favored pets. One dog was named Malcolm Hitler (as that's what the children thought Hitler's first name had been). Malcom disappeared and was probably eaten, since black dogs were considered a delicacy.

Another dog had such bad mange John appropriately named him "Scratch." Due to his scratching, he had no hair left. Kathy worked hard to feed and care for Scratch, hoping he would get better.

Dogs Cyclo and Savage joined the Banker menagerie. Savage, an inherited German Shepherd, was appropriately named since he tried to bite holes in the necks of their other canines.

GIs visiting from Camp McDermott always elicited excitement from the kids. Like fond big brothers, they allowed the schoolchildren to climb on their backs.

The children also appreciated the way their teachers really loved and cared for them. The girls spent many weekends at the home of their teacher, Miss (Janie) Voss, having late night sleep-overs. She was also a comfort and help in difficult times, living out the presence of Jesus in their lives. Miss (Karen) Gunnette spurred them on to a whole-hearted and deeper love for Jesus as she played her guitar and sang.

An Unplanned Summer (1972)

While Betty was busy overseeing much of what went on in the Children's Home, John continued with the translation of the scriptures. A young Bahnar man named Tuwari, a newer member of the translation team, came to Nha Trang to work with John in January and February 1972. After Tuwari returned home, He'i came down for most of March and April, persevering on the translation of Matthew and 1 Corinthians. Then He'i also returned to his village.

By February 1972, the Bahnar team was finishing up the drafts of the last chapters of Matthew. Tuwari had just finished reading the Book of Mark for the second time. The Bankers were waiting for the first volume of Bahnar Scriptures to be printed as a small booklet. About one half of the Bahnar New Testament was in some stage of translation.

During this time peace continued to reign in Nha Trang. In April the workshop for checking translation took place. The Millers, Haupers, and Coopers were also involved. The Millers had just finished the first draft of the Bru New Testament. So John and the others checked the Millers' translation, then returned to their own translation work. The Millers were wondering what had happened to the Bru people since the Communists now occupied their area in Quang Tri.

The teacher's guide for training in literacy that Betty was revising was ready to be sent to the printers. But all was not well in the highlands where the Bahnar lived. John and Betty prayed that the scheduled literacy workshop to train the trainers could still be held.

The first publication of Bahnar Scripture portions arrived from the printers in Hong Kong. The beautiful volume with its plastic cover and India paper contained Mark, John, Acts, 1-2 Thessalonians, 1-2 Timothy, Titus, Philemon, and the three Epistles of John.

UNSTOPPABLE!

The Bahnar storybook for first graders was also back from the printer. It was encouraging to know Bahnar believers had these portions of God's Word during these difficult days. John and Betty prayed many would find much strength and encouragement from these scriptures. And as the days passed, they were thrilled to see the Lord begin to use the newly translated Bahnar Scriptures.

Young Jonathan Gregerson, son of fellow translators Ken and Marilyn Gregerson, hurt his leg while playing outside. Although a small injury, infection set in and spread to the bone, requiring him to be admitted to the hospital for treatment. For seventeen days he lay in bed in a military hospital.

In a bed next to Jonathan lay Kreiku'a, a young Bahnar soldier, severely burned. Kreiku'a and a fellow soldier had been commanded to burn down a small dilapidated hut. They poured gasoline all over the building, inside and out. While Kreiku'a was still inside, his companion lit the fire. The building exploded in flames; Kreiku'a was trapped!

With eighty-five percent of his body burned, Kreiku'a was rushed to a hospital. Lying in that hospital bed he had one passion keeping him alive; he was determined to seek revenge.

One morning, Marilyn Gregerson came to see her son Jonathan. She brought Kreiku'a the volume of recently published Bahnar Scriptures. Kreiku'a was eager to read this book to see what God had to say about getting even with one's enemies.

UNSTOPPABLE!

Confined to his bed, Kreiku'a began reading the book of Acts about 8:30 that morning. He was still reading when his lunch came at noon. It sat unnoticed; he continued to read. Day after day he read the Bible like he was starving.

The Gregersons told him about Jesus, using the Vietnamese language. He'i, in another city, sent cassette tapes in the Bahnar language also explaining the way of salvation through faith in the Lord Jesus Christ.

What Kreiku'a was looking for was revenge. What he found was forgiveness.

One day he said to Marilyn, "This book says that it is not right to get even. I must forgive."

Soon, he asked the Lord Jesus Christ to forgive his sins, to change his heart, and help him to forgive his fellow soldier. The tape recordings made by He'i also included the hymns that he had translated. The last time Marilyn Gregerson saw the burned Bahnar soldier he was singing hymns along with the tape recorder.

Kreiku'a was released from the hospital and he went home. A fellow Bahnar believer from another village began to disciple him and soon Kreiku'a began to share his faith with the people in his own village.

Forgiving one's enemies was totally countercultural for the Bahnar. As they listened to Kreiku'a's amazing story and heard the scriptures read they too began to believe in Jesus.

UNSTOPPABLE!

Soon they built a little church out of split bamboo with round bamboo poles as "pews" and regularly gathered together to worship.[12]

Whenever the Bankers went to worship with Kreiku'a and the believers in his village, they saw Kreiku'a holding the Bible in his disfigured hands and sharing the truth of God's Word with his people.

Life was not easy for Kreiku'a. Scars covered his face and neck. His lips and neck became so cracked it was hard for him to turn his head. His hands were so deformed it was hard for him to grasp a hoe to work in the fields and provide enough for his family. Yet he continued to share with his people about how God forgives people and transforms them.

---

[12] The artwork on the cover of this book was inspired by the memory of what this little church looked like.

The number of believers in his village increased until they could no longer fit in the little bamboo church; instead they worshipped God, sitting on the ground outside. Later they were able to build a bigger building. Twenty-seven years later very few people in his village were not following the Lord.

In April 1972, Nha Trang remained peaceful, while fierce fighting raged elsewhere. U.S. forces stationed around Nha Trang kept careful watch, their numbers strengthened with troops arriving from Cam Ranh where bases were being closed. Other soldiers were returning home to the U.S.

The school year ended in May and the schoolchildren living in the Children's Home went home to be with their parents for the three-month summer vacation. The Bankers had planned to go back to Pleiku for the summer to be near the Bahnar people and continue with translation there. But they felt the Lord telling them to wait.

A week later fighting broke out again in the central highlands. Tan Canh fell. Kontum became seriously threatened and the security of Pleiku, about 30 miles to the south, was in question. The missionaries living in Pleiku had to evacuate.

UNSTOPPABLE!

John and Betty, still in Nha Trang, wrote home:

Please pray for the people in the highlands and other parts of Viet Nam who are affected by the fighting. Many have become refugees. Some have come here to Nha Trang. But many of the people, especially the tribal people, probably will not leave the highlands.

Please pray especially for the believers that their faith will be strong and through their faithfulness to the Lord many others will find that the Lord is their helper too.

We don't know what the next weeks and months hold, but we do know the Lord is still in control.

On May 7, when the Bankers came back from church, they saw the Viet Nam Christian Service Land Rover from Pleiku pulling into the VNCS clinic next door. They also thought they saw a tribal man standing by the Land Rover so they went over to investigate. To their delight, they discovered their Bahnar friends, Om and Kakni and their families, 23 people in all.

Bob Miller of VNCS in Pleiku had desired to send two of their vehicles down to Nha Trang. Since Om usually drove one, he came. Bob encouraged him to bring his family too.

Nene, who had worked for the Bankers the previous November and December also came, as well as Itelli who also previously worked with the Bankers. A blind lady and one mentally disabled one accompanied them. He'i and his family hoped to come too, if they could find a way.

The Bankers invited the group to stay at the school property with them. The first night they all slept in the little shack that had a plank floor and corrugated roofing. The next night some of their guests slept in the school. Some tried playing basketball with a hoop tied on the trunk of a coconut tree. They enjoyed the ocean, which many of them had never seen before. However, since they came from the mountains, they felt dizzy down on the coast.

The Bankers had a full "house" as Pat Bonnell was also staying for the summer at the Children's Home. She was helping out at the hospital right next door while one of the nurses was on vacation.

The volume of 12 New Testament books had come back from the printers. The Bankers studied these scriptures every night with the 23 Bahnar refugees now living with them. The Bankers were thankful that things continued to remain quiet in Nha Trang during this time.

John wrote home, not just about God's faithfulness to the Bahnar people but to other people groups as well:

> We have heard that the Stieng evangelist who saw many Stieng saved under his preaching has come out of An Loc safely, though he was wounded. He was thought to be dead by some since he had been in the hospital, and the ward he has been in was destroyed by the NVA artillery. But his parents had taken him out of the hospital because they knew it was dangerous and they had stayed in their bunker for a month and a half until the other day when about ten thousand of them were able to flee from An Loc.

Although the Bankers had not been able to go to the Bahnar that summer, the Bahnar had come to them. They remained with the Bankers for a month and a half until it was safe enough to return home. During that time "Grandma" Nene, one of the Bahnar ladies, accepted the Lord as her Savior. Later Betty remarked, "That month and a half living together in such close fellowship with our dear Bahnar friends was one of the most precious times we ever had in Viet Nam."

On June 18, the last of the Bahnar left on Air Viet Nam to return to Pleiku. Only Tuwari remained to assist with translation.

He'i and his family arrived in Nha Trang in mid-July. Despite the fierce fighting in the central highlands, He'i brought the exciting news: about 700 Bahnar Christians could be numbered in the village of Kreilawna near Pleiku. The church was really growing for which John and Betty greatly praised the Lord.

John and He'i busied themselves with translation again. They finished working over the book of Matthew and then started Romans. They also checked and revised a little tract that Gail Fleming (C&MA) was working on in Bahnar to present the Gospel in a simple manner. John wrote home regularly every week, in many letters expressing his thankfulness to God for the progress that they had been able to make.

In July 1972, 25 American soldiers had a retreat at the homes of the C&MA missionaries at the Bible School just up the hill from the Children's Home. Later these soldiers conducted a service at the chapel on the base, and at the end of that service, four of the soldiers received Christ as their Savior and five or six rededicated their lives to Christ.

A New School Year and Adventures (1972-73)

The new school year began in July. The Bankers were expecting between 13 and 18 children in the school that year. Once again, they would serve as Children's Home parents. John and Betty busily readied for the new school year. Tommy and Kathy helped by painting light blue chairs and desks. In the end, just 13 of the 18 children arrived.

Fred Donner, who lived with his wife right next door, was the business manager for the missionaries. He had attended Syracuse University and majored in forestry before serving as a forest ranger in Alaska and the Pacific Northwest. Fred turned from forestry to serve in the Air Force in Taiwan and Viet Nam, and then with Air America. He met Bev, a nurse in Da Nang, became a Christian, and married her. They now had returned to Viet Nam as missionaries.

Someone filled in for John and Betty as Children's Home parents for a short while so they could take a trip to Pleiku from mid-August to mid-September. Eugenia Johnston arrived to help conduct an adult literacy workshop for teachers in four languages: Bahnar, Jarai, Koho and Rade. Of the 128 attendees, 33 were Bahnar. One trainee was a young cadre whom they taught to use the teacher's guide they had produced.

UNSTOPPABLE!

Meanwhile, Betty continued work on the Bahnar dictionary. Om was having regular meetings in his home using the newly printed scriptures. John wrote home:

> We did enjoy our time in Pleiku, especially seeing how Om, Kakni and the other Christians were growing in faith and surpassing us in their service for the Lord Jesus. God does answer prayer as can been seen in Om's life and many others we know whom we have been remembering in prayer for many years.

After the literacy workshop, the Bankers returned to Nha Trang to their role as Children's Home parents. In September John wrote home.

> We have seven cats in all now. One mother cat and her three kittens; two orphan kittens that she took care of and one kitten that Jeannie got for her birthday from the Haupers. The two orphan kittens are pretty big now and they are supposed to live outside.
>
> Today two of them were up in the eaves trough when it was raining hard and Kathy went up and got them.

Several of those kittens became sickly and died. Kathy prayed for their lives and then mourned over their deaths.

In addition to serving as dorm parents for the Children's Home, John was again involved in another translation workshop. Many of the families involved in translation were attending.

On the weekends the missionaries regularly gathered at the Chinese restaurant overlooking the market. Warm fellowship was enjoyed around spreads of delicious food. The beautiful view of the tall, sharp mountains in the distance added to the shared pleasant experience. By the time the workshop was done, John, Jim Cooper, and Max Cobbey had checked the equivalent of one New Testament divided among 10 different languages.

For Christmas vacation, each of the school children returned home to their parents, and the Bankers returned to Pleiku. The town was quiet; no signs of war could be seen or heard.

The Bahnar church was significantly increasing in numbers and spiritual maturity, for which the Bankers thanked the Lord. They were encouraged about the regular use of the scriptures they had translated.

Celebrating Christmas with the Bahnar was a special treat for the Bankers and a time of great joy for the Bahnar. Special services were held with dramas of the Christmas story performed in the Bahnar language.

The Bankers also attended Vietnamese Christmas programs. At one such service, the Christmas tree went up in a blaze when the candles decorating the tree caught fire. The Banker children's spirits were not dampened, however. They enjoyed eating the candy treats given them at these events.

The Banker children always looked forward to these trips from the sea coast up to the mountains. The Bahnar were their "family." They reveled in all the space there was to run and play, and their favorite great banyan tree to climb. Playing hide-and-seek in its branches, a child on one side of the tree couldn't see another on the other side.

UNSTOPPABLE!

Trips to the village every weekend for church were followed by a picnic lunch. The meal finished, the children explored ravines, or climbed on the backs of cows, who until that point had been happily chewing their cud. The youngsters raced about and gingerly stepped across swinging bamboo bridges over swiftly flowing rivers. And at village church potluck dinners, they sated themselves with green deer meat and corn on the cob.

Convoys of trucks and jeeps, the sounds of artillery practice and helicopters, and the sights of bunkers and rolled barbed wire fences—all were as common place to the Banker children as McDonalds and video games are to kids in America today. The flower pots in their yard were large artillery shells, and one of their pastimes was to collect different kinds of bullet shells.

In the afternoons, while the mother tongue translators were having a rest, John read to the children for an hour or more. The Banker children's favorite stories were the J.R.R. Tolkien Middle Earth and C.S. Lewis' Narnia books.

John read those books every year for many years till they practically had them memorized. John would sit on the green couch and read while the kids listened. Simultaneously, they pretended to sneak up on their dad, creeping and crawling under the couch and atop the back of the chair.

UNSTOPPABLE!

At bedtime John metamorphosed into a Chinese. "Sam Woo" came into the children's room and with his Chinese accent entertained them with stories of his adventures.

In January 1973 the Bankers returned to Nha Trang to continue as Children's Home parents. Since He'i's wife was about to have a baby, Om accompanied the Bankers to Nha Trang to help John move ahead with the work of Bible translation. Om and John worked diligently on Luke's Gospel, endeavoring to finish by mid-March. When completed, 72.6 percent of the New Testament could be read in Bahnar.

As the school year was drawing to a close, the Bankers took the schoolchildren for a boat trip to Hon Tre, an island off the shore of Nha Trang they frequented two or three times a year. They swam at a white sandy beach, jumped off the boat repeatedly, climbed a rock face, and swam into a cave. These trips were special times each year but soon the Bankers would be moving on. The Millers would be taking over as dorm parents for the Children's Home for the next year, so the Bankers would be free to work with the Bahnar full time.

The Bankers and their children boarded the Air America flight heading for Pleiku. Because of enemy activity in the area the pilot flew low, just above the road. Above the trees the plane might be seen and shot down.

UNSTOPPABLE!

A Season of Peace and Opportunity (1973-74)

On January 27, 1973, the U.S. and North Vietnamese governments signed the Paris Peace Accord, effecting a short-lived season of peace. The NVA agreed to pull back and stop fighting and the Americans agreed to pull their troops out of Viet Nam.

As a result, Pleiku was quiet as was most of the country; in fact, the security of the Pleiku area was better than it had been for many years. The Bankers hoped to move up there for the rest of the year.

The Bankers now were allowed to go out to the Bahnar villages almost every weekend, and sometimes during the week. John was even able to go to Om's village which had never been possible before. While Tom, Kathy and Mary Alice were home for Christmas vacation the family spent a night in a village. That was the first time the children had ever slept in the village, and it was John and Betty's first overnight since 1960.

How exciting it was to see the Lord at work in Bahnar lives! During 1973, many came to know Him and others returned to the Lord. Many grew in their walk with the Lord, evidencing a real burden for those who did not yet know Jesus as their Savior. In several villages previously unreached with the gospel, people were coming to faith in Christ for the first time.

UNSTOPPABLE!

A great hunger to study the Word of God also was observed. While John was teaching a literacy training course to public schoolteachers, one of the Christian teachers was constantly reading the Bahnar Scriptures during class.

During the summer months the Bankers were busy training the Bahnar to teach their own people to read. They equipped about a hundred teachers, some to do adult literacy, some to teach elementary school children, and some to do church-based literacy. Many began teaching in the villages. John then helped to train teachers for the neighboring Sedang language.

A number of Bahnar villages dotted the countryside outside the city, beginning about eight miles away. Three or four villages were larger; several had fewer inhabitants. The villages were on higher ground than their surrounding rice fields. The view was beautiful.

UNSTOPPABLE!

Good-sized congregations were flourishing in four villages, and in at least one other a few Christians met together. The Banker family regularly participated in the Sunday service in Kreilawna, where John and Betty had lived for about three weeks when first studying Bahnar. There had been no Christians at that time; now about a hundred attended church.

The man now serving as pastor had been one of the boys who gathered to watch John and Betty in their early days studying Bahnar. He had become a Christian in 1965 and attended one year of Bible School. This was very unusual for someone from a tribal village at this time.

In August 1973, the Bankers and Om were about to leave to go to church in Domto'a village. One of the keys to the house was bent so they couldn't lock the door. Betty and the girls stayed home.

On the way Om, John and Tommy stopped by the village in which Kreiku'a, the young soldier who had been badly burned, was now pastoring. There stood a newly-built little woven bamboo church. Eleven Bahnar were gathered there. John joined them for the service, then took all 11 of them to Domto'a village for another service. When they arrived, they found the church filled with nearly 200 people.

UNSTOPPABLE!

Kreiku'a's congregation also continued to grow. On some Sundays, the Bankers joined Kreiku'a and his small congregation in the little bamboo church.

The Bankers faced much sickness the second half of the year. Betty and Nancy were hit with dengue fever, and Tommy and Mary Alice fought a flu bug.

By March 1974 about 80 percent of the Bahnar New Testament was at least in first draft. About half of this was in print and being used by the Bahnar people. The Bankers were looking to the Lord to enable them to complete the Bahnar New Testament by their furlough which was two years away. They realized that this would be impossible without the prayers of God's people.

John and Betty wrote home asking people to pray for wisdom, patience, adequate health, good Bahnar helpers, a minimum of interruptions, and victory over hindrances to getting God's Word to the Bahnar.

The security in the Bahnar area was deteriorating again. The Bankers wrote home asking for prayer for the protection of the Bahnar. "Pray that the Lord would overrule," they said, "so that the door would stay open and His Word would continue to spread."

UNSTOPPABLE!

In March 1974 the Bankers returned to Nha Trang for another translation workshop. John was very busy as he had the responsibility of directing the workshop, teaching seminars, and checking translation that their fellow workers had done.

Tuwari, a young Bahnar fellow, was helping Betty translate. Betty wrote:

> We trust this will be a time of real spiritual growth in Tuwari's life. Pray that his parents will be saved. Life is very hard for the Bahnar Christian young people whose parents are unbelievers.

As He'i translated God's Word into his own language, God's Holy Spirit was transforming his life. While working on Romans, He'i said, "How did Paul know so much about me? I'm just like this!"

At times he had such a great burden for the spiritual needs of his own people that he could hardly wait to take the newly translated portions home to his village to share with the growing church there.

When he got to Hebrews, he became very excited, "This is just what my people need. The sacrifice has already been made. There is no need for the Bahnar to make any more sacrifices!"

UNSTOPPABLE!

A Different Sort of Evacuation (1974)

After the translation workshop, the Bankers returned to Pleiku, working toward their goal of finishing the Bahnar New Testament. The children were excited to finish the school year in Nha Trang and fly home to Pleiku for the summer.

One day, Kathy fell from a rope swing, hit the back of her head and passed out from a concussion. When John saw his daughter was unconscious, his concern was so great that he also fainted. By the time the doctor arrived, Kathy had already regained consciousness, but the doctor was concerned for John who took longer to come to.

Not long after, news reached the Bankers in Pleiku that one of their children's school friends fell out of a tree, hit her head on concrete, and died. Fear of death encompassed 12-year-old Kathy; she couldn't shake it. She sought help from her mother. She needed to make sure if she, too, died, she would go to heaven.

Kathy prayed with Betty, again confirming Jesus as her Savior. A peace seeped into Kathy's heart and filled her whole being. She basked in that blissful peace for days until it gradually faded, but the fear that had gripped her previously did not return. Little did she know that death would soon come looking for her.

With summer vacation ended, the children returned to school on the coast for the fall semester of 1974. Little Nancy was starting school for the first time. On her September birthday she fell, hitting her leg on a steel divider that anchored the teeter-totter in place. She was rushed off to have the wound cleansed, but a large knot was already bulging. Her spirits undampened, Nancy soon was bouncing around as usual. Then the pain set in accompanied by a fever. An x-ray at the clinic next door revealed no broken bones, but the growing infection required a penicillin shot. The infection worsened, growing red and full of pus. Hot compresses were applied.

Accompanied by her older sister Kathy, Nancy was hurried again to the clinic to have her leg lanced. She lay on a hospital table surrounded by the doctor and nurses. Kathy stood behind the table against the wall—a big sister in her motherly role.

As the needle pierced Nancy's leg she screamed. Pus gushed out. Kathy disappeared. *Where had she gone?* They found her a couple seconds later. She had fainted at her sister's scream, slid down the wall and fell crumpled to the floor. Thankfully, the lancing did the trick and Nancy's leg began to heal.

About a month later, the youngsters were rushing around excitedly getting their bathing suits and towels ready for another great boat trip to the nearby island of Hon Tre.

Kathy wanted desperately to go, but now she was the one who felt so ill. Doing her best to ignore it, she pretended she wasn't sick, but it was no use. The pain in her side was all encompassing to the point that she could not even pretend.

In the next couple of days many of the other children in the Children's Home fell sick. Lying in their bunk beds, one above the other, they took turns groaning and moaning. The doctor from the clinic next door came and diagnosed everyone, including Kathy, with hepatitis. It was almost a fatal mistake.

The other children did indeed have hepatitis, but the pain that Kathy was feeling was much more severe and different. Further examinations indicated that she had appendicitis! The nearby clinic was unequipped to handle the problem so plans were set in motion to find a way to get her down to Saigon for the medical help she urgently needed.

Fred Donner, who lived next door to the school, rushed to town to find a USAID doctor and a plane to evacuate her to Saigon. But this was no small matter.

Precious time elapsed as Kathy sat in the Children's Home waiting for help to come. But she felt no fear, only a deep sense of calm. A fellow student said to her, "I can't understand how all this is happening to you, yet you are at peace!"

When Fred finally returned, Kathy was driven to the airport and he boarded the medevac flight with her to Saigon. A half hour after the plane left, a great storm rolled in. The plane had departed just in time.

In the plane, Kathy lay on a stretcher. She watched the people traveling with her as they looked out the window and made comments about the stars.

Upon landing in Saigon, Kathy was rushed by ambulance to the hospital. Just as they were wheeling her into the operation room in the 3rd Field Hospital, the pain disappeared. Her appendix had burst!

UNSTOPPABLE!

Up in the central highlands of Pleiku, John and Betty had gone as usual to church in the village. Suddenly someone from Air America rushed in. "Your daughter has been medevacked to Saigon with appendicitis!" he exclaimed.

They immediately hurried back to the city and desperately tried to board a flight for Saigon. Flight after flight took off, but there was no room.

In grave concern they returned to the C&MA compound and gathered with those there to pray. At this time God brought to Betty's mind the story of the 12-year-old girl whom Jesus raised from the dead. Kathy, too, was 12 years old!

Unbeknownst to John and Betty, the head surgeon from a medical training school in California was providentially visiting the hospital in Saigon at that time. Kathy was wheeled into O.R. for the surgery which was needed immediately. But the doctor still could not operate; Kathy's temperature had soared dangerously high. They lay her on an ice-cold table desperately trying to get her fever to come down a few degrees.

When the surgeon finally cut into Kathy's abdomen, they found the poison had already spread through her body. Were they too late?

They poured penicillin into her body, not knowing that her parents believed Kathy was allergic to it. Laying on the operating table Kathy wandered in dark dreams. She found herself walking through a dark tunnel toward the other end.

UNSTOPPABLE!

After a day or two, John and Betty were able to catch a flight to Saigon. Upon arrival, they headed straight for the hospital and asked for Kathy. To their great concern no one knew where she was.

Finally, they found two single missionaries who had been taking turns staying by her side in the Intensive Care Unit of the American military hospital.[13] They told John and Betty that the prognosis was not good. Though she survived the surgery, she was still in a critical condition.

Slowly but surely, Kathy began to recover. Eventually she was able to return to school, though still bent over because of the pain.

John and Betty rejoiced in God's faithfulness and giving the gift of life to their eldest daughter. God had a purpose and plan for Kathy's life that a burst appendix couldn't stop.

No Human Plan (1975-77)

Other rejoicing was also around the corner. On December 27, 1974 John and Betty wrote home:

> Our hearts are full of special praise to the Lord for His faithfulness. On December 5th we finished translating the first draft of the Bahnar New Testament in the Pleiku dialect. It has been a long and difficult task, and we could never have done it apart from the Lord's enabling and your faithfulness in praying for us and supporting and encouraging us through the years.

---

[13] The U.S. Army 3rd field hospital became the 7th Day Adventist hospital.

UNSTOPPABLE!

We thank the Lord for He'i, our main translation helper, who has faithfully worked with us the past seven years. However, the task is NOT FINISHED! We have much checking and revising to do. First, we plan to check through the translation with other Bahnar to make sure that it is understandable to those who have not helped translate it. Then from mid-February through early May we plan to attend a translation workshop in Nha Trang where translation consultants will check the translation. After we return to Pleiku in May, we will begin another check with Bahnar church leaders.

Please pray that all the checking and preparation for printing may be finished by the scheduled time for our furlough in late spring, 1976, so that the Bahnar New Testament may be submitted for printing at that time.

We thank the Lord for progress in literacy too. Betty and Nid, a Bahnar school teacher, are making good progress on the new Bahnar primer and teacher's guide. Betty has a reading class of about 20 Bahnar children to test out the new primer. And there are encouraging reports from the Bahnar literacy classes in the public schools, the adult literacy classes and church related literacy programs. One Bahnar pastor has about 85 people learning to read in the four congregations he is responsible for.

Most of the Bahnar churches are growing. However, we request special prayer for the church in the largest

UNSTOPPABLE!

Bahnar village, Kreilawna. Attendance is about half what it used to be and there is much opposition to the believers in that village.

Joy filled their hearts, but the battle was still fierce. Upheavals were approaching of which the Bankers never dreamt. After a time of spiritual refreshment and growing together with their fellow missionaries in the highland city of Dalat, they and many of their colleagues began yet another translation workshop in Nha Trang. Little did they know that this may have saved many of their lives.

An all-out battle spread through the central highland town of Ban Me Thuot early in the morning of March 10, 1975 while the Bankers and their colleagues were in Nha Trang. The fighting ended a few days later with the Communist forces in full control.

John and Carolyn Miller and their five-year-old daughter were trapped. They had been putting in the final touches of the Bru New Testament and were nearly ready to send it off to the printer. Advancing NVA soldiers discovered them along with five C&MA missionaries and took them captive.

After the fall of Ban Me Thuot, and the dwindling presence of the American military, the situation in the rest of the highlands fell apart rapidly. On March 17 Pleiku fell.

UNSTOPPABLE!

As the situation in Viet Nam continued to deteriorate the Bankers and other missionaries in Nha Trang were advised to evacuate to Saigon. There were now one million refugees fleeing from the highlands, many of them coming to Nha Trang. The roads were crowded with vehicles. The Bridge at Tuy Hoa was blown up; thousands were stranded.

Betty and her children, along with the other missionary wives and children, flew to Saigon on March 24. John remained in Nha Trang with the other husbands to close down their office and properties and hand them over to the national evangelical church. Pastor An arrived in Nha Trang along with orphans from the Jeh language group. They stayed in the children's school for three days.

The NVA was advancing. Time was short. Planning to join their families in Saigon on the 29th, the men worked tirelessly. Some hoped to leave in the morning and others in the afternoon.

Just before noon on the 29th they received a message instructing them to get to the consulate as soon as possible. Nha Trang was quickly becoming less and less secure. Refugees were flooding into the city, fleeing their home areas, and there was much unrest afoot.

Quickly obeying the command, John was one of the first to arrive at the consulate. Whisked by bus to the airport, they found a 727 jet on the tarmac, readying for takeoff.

Their hearts sank into their stomachs. The plane was full of people fleeing for their lives; only a few from the bus could get on!

UNSTOPPABLE!

John and the others waited and waited while the jet flew to Saigon. When it finally returned, they gratefully boarded and flew to the capital city where John met up with his family.

A few days later Nha Trang, a city now in chaos, fell to the Communists.

In Saigon, even the children helped shut down operations. A large fire blazed, burning paperwork and records. Although an intense time for the adults, Tommy, Kathy, Mary Alice and Nancy thought this was all a great adventure. [This lack of fear was evidence of God's grace upon them despite all they had experienced in their short lives. Their parent's constant unrelenting faith in God carried them too.] They were so excited! No room was available for them at the missionary group house, so they had the special privilege of sleeping on the 8th floor of the Oscar hotel and eating at the Brinks Hotel restaurant nearby!

As the situation in Viet Nam and Cambodia continued to deteriorate, the missionaries fled to other countries. The Bankers and a number of their colleagues evacuated to the Philippines on April 1, 1975.

On April 4 a USAF C5A crashed with orphans aboard. Vivian Clark and Laurie Stark were killed. From the top of the missionary group house and office building, one of the children's teachers, Janie Voss, sadly watched the smoke rising from the fallen plane; It was heartbreaking.

UNSTOPPABLE!

The next day, April 5, Janie herself was to board a plane with orphans, ranging from infants to eight-year-olds. Janie Voss, Jackie Maier, Clinton Prairie, Dave and Marlene Lawrence and many others accompanied 350 Vietnamese orphans flying to the U.S. where American families were waiting to provide a welcoming home for each of them.

Janie's responsibilities were the 17 babies in the front rows of seats located under the cockpit of the 747 aircraft. Some of the babies in their bassinets were strapped into seats and other bassinets were located under the seats. Having no seat for the takeoffs and landings, Janie sat in the aisle with her back to the front wall of the cabin. An open barrel stood in the aisle, full of dirty diapers. The smell overwhelmed the escorts as well as the new crews that stepped on the flights in Guam and Hawaii.

At these stops Red Cross workers also came on board so Janie and the other escorts could get off the plane for a brief time.

The older children were served hamburgers during the flight, a totally unknown food to these rice and vegetable eaters.

Chicken pox broke out along the way; the upper lounge of the 747 became the isolation ward. One emaciated baby boy was too weak to drink from the bottle. Then he disappeared. Janie was very concerned. *Had his little life been snuffed out?* Upon arrival in Seattle, the loudspeaker announced each of the children had survived the flight. It was a miracle!

UNSTOPPABLE!

Before the flight continued on to other cities, all the children disembarked in Seattle. They were taken to a large room where mattresses lined the floor. With no inoculation records, all the children received the necessary shots. The cacophony of 350 crying children was overwhelming.

Janie and Jackie accompanied the flight on as far as Chicago where they were met by Ralph and Lorraine Haupers, who were on furlough that year. What a blessing to be with colleagues who understood the strong emotions they were feeling and the deep sense of loss, knowing they could never go back to Viet Nam and to all they loved.

On April 8th the last of the Bankers' colleagues, five men[14] and Dave and Dot Thomas, left the country. Their properties, now in the hands of the Evangelical Church of Viet Nam, were to be used to house Christian refugees. That same day the presidential palace was bombed and a 24-hour curfew instituted.

Refugees were evacuated by the tens of thousands from Viet Nam before the country fell. On April 30, 1975, the last American climbed on board the last helicopter out of Saigon, an act that marked the end of America's official military presence in Viet Nam.

In the Philippines the Bankers and the other evacuees were taken in by colleagues, just as they had been seven years previously after the '68 Tet offensive. Three teachers from the children's school in Viet Nam evacuated together

---

[14] These men were Richard Pittman, Dick Watson, Ken Gregerson, Milt Barker and Bob Mckee.

UNSTOPPABLE!

with the rest of the group and continued to teach the children till the end of the school year.

Every morning, the whole group met to pray for the Millers and other missionaries who were captured and remained in Viet Nam. They interceded as well for the people from the many language groups whom they dearly loved and with whom their lives were intertwined.

Betty wrote home:

> The future?? It is unknown. But we know the One who knows the future and we rest in Him, knowing that He never makes mistakes. He is not just over-ruling, but He is ruling!
>
> Please pray for the Bahnar Christians in Viet Nam and the many other believers there, who are going through very deep waters now. Pray that they will be faithful to the Lord no matter what it costs, and that many others will find their help in the Lord during these difficult days.
>
> Pray too that the Lord will make a way for us to finish the Bahnar New Testament and then get it to the Bahnar. They have about 38 percent of the New Testament in print so far.

UNSTOPPABLE!

At this time the number of Bahnar believers had grown to around 1,000. Eight months later, as 1975 came to an end, Betty wrote again:

> These have been months of learning for us—learning in God's school. We have learned much about the sovereignty of God, not just in our own lives but in the lives of our friends left in Viet Nam as well. God has been reminding us of His great faithfulness to us in each area of our lives and teaching us that He is no less faithful to His children in Viet Nam.
>
> So, we must not sorrow for them, but rejoice that God is working out His perfect plan in their lives right now. What more could we ask?

During those months John and Betty continued to work on the Bahnar New Testament and other Bahnar language materials. At first John struggled to find the motivation he needed to finish. He found it hard to do the final editing without a Bahnar speaker to help. And it seemed impossible that the New Testament would ever get to the Bahnar. *Was it worth it?*

Grief for the country and its people filled his heart. And knowing those he loved were now suffering only deepened John's depression.

UNSTOPPABLE!

A colleague suggested that John produce scripture radio programs in the Bahnar language to encourage the people, but at first, he did not want to do this. He felt his reading of the Bahnar Scripture with an English accent would be too unnatural and therefore difficult for Bahnar people to understand.

As John struggled in this way, the Lord strengthened his heart to persevere. In answer to prayer, the Lord provided someone to type the Bahnar New Testament, preparing it for printing and publication.

Ruth Phelps was willing to do the job. After retiring from 35 years of secretarial work, she had responded to the Lord's call to help get His Word to those without it. She had previously served for five years in Viet Nam, and now returned from the U.S. again to type the Bahnar and other Scriptures for publication.

The missionary "refugees" in the Philippines continued to pray day in and day out, month in and month out, for their friends captured by the Communists. Finally, after seven and a half months of captivity in Viet Nam, John and Carolyn Miller were released along with their six-year-old LuAnne. On their way back to the U.S. to join their three other children, they stopped in the Philippines to share firsthand their experiences in captivity with their colleagues.[15]

[f15] You can read the full account of the Miller's story in Carolyn's book, *Captured!* (Miller, 1977).

UNSTOPPABLE!

The Bankers and others listened in amazement as they heard how God had answered their prayers for the Millers and their hearts were strengthened. God had taken care of the Millers through sickness, frequent moves from camp to camp, interrogations, sorrow due to separation from their other children and the Bru people they loved, and sorrow at the loss of the final draft of the New Testament that they had finished for publication just before they were captured. This was the loss of their life's work and the Bru's dream of having God's Word in their language.

While still in prison camp the Millers had been interrogated to find what wrongs they had committed. They were questioned about their motives in coming to Viet Nam. Carolyn answered, "The Bible is the most precious thing we have because we believe it is God's Word. We felt we must share it with the people of the minority languages of Viet Nam who don't have it." In one session they were scolded:

> You've come over to Viet Nam and you've gone to these tribal people and taught them about God. Many of them have left their sacrificing to the spirits and they've believed. They will remember you! Every time they read the Bible you've translated, they'll remember you. Every time they use the alphabet you've prepared, they'll remember you. Furthermore, they'll tell their children

about you. And their children will tell their children. It will be many years before what you have done will disappear!

These words meant to discourage and condemn brought great encouragement to Carolyn instead. Furthermore, God hadn't forgotten the Bru people's dream of having God's Word in their own language. When the Millers arrived in the Philippines, they discovered that Ruth Phelps had stayed in Saigon till the very last moment. She typed up everything, making back-up copies of the precious work of the translators. These precious scriptures had been preserved! The Millers would again undertake the careful process of preparing the Bru Scriptures for publication.

John and Betty had not been able to communicate with the Bahnar since leaving Viet Nam but John began to produce radio programs. Thirty-minute tape recordings of Bahnar Scripture and hymns were broadcast over shortwave radio by the Far East Broadcasting Company (FEBC) in Manila. These broadcasts contained the portions of scripture that the Bahnar did not yet have in print.

The Bankers earnestly prayed that the Bahnar would have opportunities to listen to these scripture recordings, and have batteries for their radios. They asked the Lord to use these tapes to encourage and strengthen the believers and also reach those who still did not know Him.

Meanwhile, John and Betty moved forward with the painstaking process of putting in all the finishing touches to the Bahnar New Testament. They too were very thankful for the help of Ruth Phelps.

UNSTOPPABLE!

In May 1976 they left the finished copy of the Bahnar New Testament at the printer in Manila! That document was the fruit of many years of hard labor against so many obstacles. Yet while they headed to the U.S. for a year's furlough, the spiritual battle still raged on.

A few months later the distressing news reached them in the U.S. that in July a blazing fire had consumed the Philippine printshop. The print-ready copy of the Bahnar New Testament was destroyed, burned to ashes! In an instant their many years of hard, painstaking, sacrificial work had gone up in smoke.

And now there was no way to go back to Viet Nam to start again. That door was firmly shut. Personal computers did not yet exist so there was no readily accessible back-up copy to be instantly retrieved. However, they had kept a carbon copy. Ruth Phelps, who had typed the previous manuscript for printing, immediately volunteered to type it again from the carbon copy backup!

UNSTOPPABLE!

Seven months later, in January 1977, she finished typing the Bahnar New Testament for the second time. It was sent to a printer for publication.

Despite the fierce fighting, separation, captivity (even death) for some, fire, loss, much sorrow and many tears, God's grand purpose to provide His Word to the Bahnar and other peoples of Viet Nam was unstoppable.

God Moving Through Closed Doors (1977-79)

Now that it was printed, how would they ever get the New Testament to the Bahnar people who were now living in a closed country? Surely God would make a way—*but when and how*?

With no possibility for the Bankers to return to Viet Nam, they prayed about what God would have them do following their furlough. They felt God might be calling them to do Bible translation with another Bibleless people group, either in Thailand or Sabah, East Malaysia.

Since permission had not yet been granted in Thailand, and none of their colleagues had yet gone to Sabah, they took a temporary assignment in the Philippines as house parents in Nasuli. They would again be taking care of missionary children in school, enabling their parents to continue their work in rural communities.

During this time, they recorded more radio programs of Bahnar Scripture reading and hymns. They produced twenty-six 15-minute programs. Each program was broadcast every Friday evening. Every evening 30 minutes of scripture were broadcast in a different language each day of the week. The Bankers had not yet heard news from any Bahnar so they continued to pray and broadcast in faith.

A friend and colleague, Janice Saul, received letters from another ethnic group who said they were listening to the programs in their language. The Bankers felt that some Bahnar must be listening too. They hoped to make more tapes in the new year for continued broadcasting.

The first printing of 500 copies of the Bahnar New Testament came off the press in October 1977. The dedication of the New Testament was held on December 4 at Nasuli, Philippines. John and Betty told of the many wonderful ways the Lord had worked to cause the Bahnar New Testament to become a reality. Their director, Ken Smith, shared about getting the scripture into the hands of the Bahnar. Then everyone joined in prayer that the Lord would accomplish His purposes through the Bahnar Scriptures.

UNSTOPPABLE!

While Bankers served as Children's Home parents. John wrote home:

> Betty is especially busy with the work here in the Children's Home. For the last couple of weeks, we have had 12 children. That is the most we have had so far. It keeps one busy trying to keep them happy away from their parents...seeking to help in their spiritual growth.
>
> We appreciate your prayers for this part of our ministry. I have been doing a little translation checking here. During the last six weeks or so there has been a translation workshop and I checked Romans, Colossians and Hebrews, each in a different language.

After a year serving as house parents for missionary children, the Bankers moved to Manila. They served in their Asia Area office, awaiting a visa to move to Sabah, Malaysia. In December 1978 John wrote home:

> There are over two thousand Vietnamese refugees living in a refugee center near our home here in Manila. All of them have crossed the thousand miles of ocean between Viet Nam and the Philippines, many in small fishing boats. They will stay in this refugee center until sponsors can be found for them and permission granted for them to settle in the United States, Canada or some other western country. The Lord has given us a ministry to them through teaching English twice a week at which time we also have opportunity to share the Word of God with them. Please pray for this ministry.
>
> One of the refugees is a Bahnar friend of ours who helped us make primers in the mid-60s. He accepted the Lord Jesus Christ as his Savior in July. Pray that he will fully understand what this means and commit his life

completely to the Lord. He will be going to the Boston area soon. Pray for his wife and five small children, still in Viet Nam, that they will somehow be able to join him.

Continue to remember the suffering church in Viet Nam. We have heard that about 100 evangelical churches have been closed, including those in the Bahnar area, and 90 pastors have been arrested. One or two Bahnar New Testaments have reached Saigon. But it is very difficult to get them to the Bahnar people in the highlands. The Bahnar radio programs continue to go out each Friday.

About a year later, in October 1979, John again wrote:

As we begin a new work [in Sabah, Malaysia] please continue to remember the Bahnar church in Viet Nam and the Christians in Viet Nam in general. A Christian refugee who left Viet Nam a little over a month ago has brought fresh glimpses of the church there. He verifies that all churches in the Bahnar area have been closed.

We were glad to hear that some Vietnamese pastor friends of ours are alive and well. He had no knowledge of any of the Bahnar, but he has seen the young Vietnamese missionary to the Bahnar, though not recently.

He told us that pastors who are arrested often go to prison which is much more confining than re-education camps. It is a sobering thought that some of our friends may be in prison.

Indeed, many were trying to escape Viet Nam at this time. One boat of about 40 people ran out of food and water as they floated between Viet Nam and the Philippines.

Occasional rain kept them alive until their boat finally shipwrecked on a white sandy beach on the island of Caluya.

Kermit Titrud, a Bible Translator, met them there. For around a month he told them about God's Word. Some of them believed in Jesus.

After the Philippine government moved the refugees to Manila, Kermit found them again and spent time fellowshipping and worshipping with them. He called John to come join them as he was not sure what their prayers were about and to whom they were praying, since he didn't speak Vietnamese or any language of Viet Nam.

John joined in their time of worship. He assured Kermit that they were indeed praying to God out of true hearts of faith.

Sow your Seed in the Morning and in the Evening Don't be Idle (1979-98)

Making God's Word available to as many people as possible continued to be John and Betty's heart's desire. But the ways they pursued this passion continued to expand and grow. In 1979 the Banker family moved to Sabah, Malaysia, where for several years they helped a new advance by conducting a survey of the languages and Bible translation needs.

In 1983, due to the increasing needs of John's elderly parents, the Bankers moved back to the U.S. Because John knew that the believers in Vietnam would now be facing prison, a burden to minister to and pray for prisoners grew in

UNSTOPPABLE!

his heart. John joined with others leading Bible studies in Dannemora's maximum security prison in Upstate New York. Betty led the Christian Youth Crusaders (CYC) ministry for children of their community. Some of those attending were prisoners' children.

Meanwhile, John and Betty pursued advanced training in Greek which would help them train and consult for others doing Bible translation. In the mid-80s, John worked with the Vietnamese Bible Translation Committee which was producing a new translation into Vietnamese.

As the years passed, John and Betty stepped into other roles furthering the task of Bible translation. In the mid-90s, John was the consultant for the Translator's Notes series being developed in Vietnamese. This was a Bible commentary series especially produced to help mother-tongue speakers translating the Bible into their own languages. In addition, John and Betty produced a training manual for equipping these mother-tongue translators in translation principles.

Over the course of 25 years John helped to author the premier commentary series for Bible translators called the *Semantic and Structural Analyses* (SSA).

UNSTOPPABLE!

In time he became the chief editor. Each SSA was an analysis of the Greek text of a New Testament book and dealt with specific problems that Bible translators encounter when translating. It incorporated all the insights of biblical scholarship and knowledge of New Testament Greek. During this time John took occasional trips to North Carolina to work with other members of the Semantic Structure Analysis team.

Betty also served in their International Translation Department in Dallas. Eventually she became the administrative assistant to the International Translation Coordinator. Her job included helping to organize Greek seminars and other Bible translation conferences. She responded to many requests and inquiries from around the world.

For many years no one outside of Viet Nam knew whether the Bahnar New Testaments the Bankers published years before had ever reached the central highlands where the people lived. Yet a copy did make its way to its destination and many copies of it were made to give to people.

Unaware of this, in faith, for many years the Bankers made radio programs that were aired in Viet Nam. The Bankers recorded the scripture themselves, read them aloud and sent them over the airwaves.

On the other side of the ocean, people heard the recordings and said, "Quick, Grandfather is on the radio. Come, let's listen!" They would gather in the homes of those who had shortwave radios.

UNSTOPPABLE!

The Bankers made these radio programs themselves for many years until some Bahnar arrived in the U.S. as refugees. Then the radio programs were made and read by Bahnar speakers themselves.

Years before when John and Betty were still in Viet Nam they had been asked to be involved in government-supported literacy classes to teach Bahnar teachers how to use primers to teach children and adults how to read their language. At the end of one of these workshops, they gave one of the books of scripture to each of the teachers who had participated in the literacy classes.

Many years later, one of those teachers wrote to the Bankers to say that he had become a Christian through reading this book of scripture. He later became the pastor of the Bahnar church in his village.

After Viet Nam fell in 1975, the new regime attempted to confiscate every single copy of scripture. However, these scriptures were so precious to the people that the one or two copies not found and destroyed were copied over and over again until the originals were dog-eared and falling apart.

For seven years, the Bankers heard no word from Viet Nam. Finally, in 1982 word came that while in prison, the Bahnar pastors' faith had been refined. They came out of prison filled with the Holy Spirit, now better equipped to both evangelize and disciple the church. Although persecution was severe, the number of believers was multiplying.

Wokni, who had been the first Bahnar believer, had been tied together with his son and led through the village, as the villagers watched and sobbed.

One night in prison, Jesus appeared to Wokni, comforting his heart with the words, "I will never leave you nor forsake you." While still in prison, Wokni led 100 people to the Lord and baptized them!

In the early 1990s a desire began to grow in Betty's heart to help translate the Old Testament for the Bahnar people. On the other side of the world, a Bahnar man named Yohansi had been trying to translate the Book of Psalms by himself for 10 years. Then in 1998, 23 years after Bankers fled from Viet Nam, requests began to come from the Bahnar church officially asking for help in Old Testament translation.

Yohansi wrote to John and Betty:

> We always remember you. When I saw your picture...I immediately prayed thanking God for choosing you to help us Bahnar people be saved from the evil spirits, from the darkness of Satan. You studied the Bahnar language then went immediately on to translating God's Word, the book in which He promises to deliver us from hell.

> In your present teaching on the radio, it is as if you were here as you used to be—we really miss you. I have kept on listening to you since the beginning—my wife and I anxiously listened, and invited many believers to listen also, and then we met together praying like you taught.

> Oh, grandfather and grandmother, regarding the seed that you have sown, it has now sprouted in villages everywhere. I watch over/care for the believers.

UNSTOPPABLE!

The day we parted I wanted to shake hands to say goodbye but there was no opportunity. Your house was all closed up, you were nowhere to be seen.

At present whoever we meet asks where you are and will a letter reach you. They no longer see your face, only hear your voice speaking and see the book you prepared.

Finally, now we have a hymnal, we truly thank the Lord. He is saving us Bahnar….Will you help us continue to translate the Bible?

Oh, grandfather and grandmother, I ask you to pray much for me, so that I will have a fluent mouth and a sharp mind, a heart of love for the Bahnar, willingly giving myself to the Lord to do His work on this earth. If it means hardship for my body I will still keep going; if it means destruction for my body, I will give my body to glorify our Lord Jesus Christ.

Pastor Kreiku'a also wrote saying, "There is an Old Testament in the national language, but I cannot understand it. Would you please do all you can so that we can have the Old Testament in our language."

There was a great need for trained leadership in the Bahnar church. Pastor Wokni had died. He and his wife had been the only believers among the Bahnar for many years. They had witnessed for almost 50 years, believing God would give fruit if they faithfully sowed the Seed.

At the time of Wokni's death he was the only ordained pastor serving 10,000 Bahnar believers. When the non-Christians in his village saw how much Christians from both near and far demonstrated their love to him and his family during his sickness and death, 50 more people from his home village turned to the Lord.

Now that he was gone, the Bahnar were trying to train themselves the best they could. Twenty men were committed to serving as pastors, with over a hundred studying a correspondence lay workers' course. But they were begging for help for Bible translation.

By the time John and Betty began to help, Yohansi had already organized a Bible translation committee. The Bahnar couldn't wait to get more of the scriptures in their language. They had the New Testament and now they wanted the Old!

A man from another ethnic minority group had also been trying to translate the New Testament for his people, but he was having such a difficult time that he decided to write a letter pleading for help. He addressed it to "any organization, any church, any group" and gave it to a man visiting his country. Somehow, that letter actually found its way to John and Betty Banker!

So, John and Betty began to train the Bahnar translation committee and others in translation principles. There were no commentaries in their language to help them understand what the original languages of the Bible said, and there were very few in Vietnamese either. John and Betty produced materials in Vietnamese to help the translators understand the meaning of the scriptures they were translating.

People from several neighboring languages were wanting to use the Bahnar New Testament as a resource to help them translate the Bible in their own languages. John and Betty trained the translation committees, and then the committees went home and drafted the scriptures into their language. The Bankers then prepared for the next checks based on what they thought the translation teams might draft by the next year and would need to have checked.

Each year the translation committees learned principles through the books they had just translated and then applied them to the books that they drafted the next year. They began by drafting Jonah, then they did Genesis and from there worked their way through the Old Testament. The translation committees wanted to work on the minor prophets early on since the message of these books really spoke to their hearts because of the persecution they were experiencing.

John and Betty's work with the Bahnar Old Testament was expanded such that they were now helping eight different languages in different stages of translating the Bible. Tears flowed down Betty's face after she heard all the stories of the tremendous price the believers had suffered for the sake of the Gospel. Betty said:

> We consider ourselves dedicated to the Lord, but we found out that we haven't even begun to learn what dedication means!

At this time the church in Viet Nam was going through a very hard time because of their faith. Even so, it continued to grow and reach out to its own people.

The church also had a real concern for other Christians around the world who were being persecuted. In the fall of

UNSTOPPABLE!

1998, during the International Day of Prayer for the Persecuted Church, some 200 believers from various congregations in Viet Nam fasted and prayed for three days for other Christians enduring persecution around the world.

God at Work in the Darkness (1999-2008)

In the late 1990s, Tsedu and his wife came to Dallas for training. He wanted to translate the Old Testament for the 300,000 speakers of his language. Years previously in Viet Nam, when Tsedu was four months old, he was accidentally dropped. Though feared dead, he was rushed to the hospital.

To everyone's surprise, the doctors were able to revive Tsedu. But, as a young child, he never spoke. His family thought that he would be a mute for life. Then to everyone's amazement, he learned to talk.

Tsedu was bothered by spirits so much that he was on the way either to becoming a sorcerer or being destroyed by the spirits. One day, while he was still young, he heard the gospel message and decided to follow Jesus. After that the oppression from the spirit world ceased.

As a young man Tsedu fearlessly shared his faith despite persecution. His name was on the wanted list. One day, after preaching he escaped through the window when alerted of trouble.

While still a young man, Tsedu became ill with a brain tumor. He lay in the hospital for 30 days and watched several other young men die who had been admitted after him. The doctor told him that even if he survived, he would lose two-thirds of his brain capacity.

During this time, Tsedu read Proverbs in Vietnamese and was blessed by it. He decided to translate Proverbs into his language. When others saw that he was able to do this they encouraged him to keep translating, saying, "If you can do this with a brain tumor, you can also translate the rest of the books of the Old Testament."

God miraculously spared Tsedu's life; not only that, his brain still worked clearly!

In time, Tsedu came to the United States to study at Taccoa Falls Bible College. During this time, he was encouraged to talk to John Banker. He called John and said, "I feel that God wants me to translate the Bible for my people. But I feel very unsure how to do it!"

John answered, "Just come over."

Tsedu said, "How can I do that?"

John replied, "Come over and stay with us." And so Tsedu and his wife did.

While Tsedu and his wife lived with the Bankers, John began the task of training Tsedu to do Bible translation. Tsedu later said, "John never told me how long it was going to take. If he had told me I would take 13 years to do the Old Testament I might never have done it."

After John trained Tsedu, he helped to check his translation. Later on, Dave Blood and then Ernie Lee took over this important responsibility for John.

UNSTOPPABLE!

Many years previously, Hank and Vange Blood had begun Bible translation in another one of the language groups in Viet Nam. At that time a boy named Muodi, whose father was a pastor, came to work for them. He did household chores, swept the floor, did the dishes and took care of their children. But one day he ran away.

During the Chinese New Year, Tet 1968, Hank was captured along with Betty Olsen and Mike Benge. Of the three only Mike ever returned home, and only after four years in captivity. Translation of the Bible into Muodi's language stopped.

In time Muodi grew up, became a Christian and later a pastor. Twenty years after Hank died in the jungle, a great movement of the Lord came upon the highland areas in that part of the country. An evangelist from a neighboring people group preached and served among Muodi's people. Things were going well!

Then the evangelist was arrested and imprisoned for 10 years. The 200 believers were severely persecuted and many of them became weak in their faith. After the evangelist was released from prison, a revival broke out and the Lord again worked in a powerful way among those people. Sadly, the evangelist died three months later.

But the seed that died bore fruit. The Lord anointed the evangelist's crippled daughter with a double portion of the same vision and power that her father had received. God gave her the ability to speak a language she had never studied and used her to heal the sick and perform other miracles.

UNSTOPPABLE!

Many people, even those antagonistic to the gospel came to know the Lord Jesus through her ministry. The church among that minority people revitalized and grew to number 7,000 believers.

Muodi longed for the day when they would have a Bible in their language. He and a couple other pastors went to get training and then started a translation team. They begged John and Betty to teach them how to translate the scriptures for the growing church among their people.

When Pastor Muodi saw John and Betty, he said, "When I was a teenager, I ate a meal in your home, and I took your daughter for rides on the back of the bicycle."

Pastor Muodi told John and Betty with great sadness that not only had Hank been taken captive and died, but because of Hank's death, his people had lost the opportunity to have the scriptures in their language.

For a number of years Hank's widow, Vange, worked on translating the Bible into Muodi's language while living in the Philippines. Talla and his wife went to work with her but then they returned to Viet Nam. Shortly after arriving home Talla was arrested and held captive in the jungle. When he tried to escape, he was killed.

Pastor Muodi told John and Betty how discouraging it was for him and his people to have lost yet another opportunity to have the scriptures in their language. He said, "Now finally after so many years we have another opportunity. We have waited so long."

UNSTOPPABLE!

The number of believers continued to increase among this people group, with now 8,000 believers among a people group of 13,000.

Hank's words spoken so many years previously were coming true:

> Let's all remember that this is not the end of the story. This is a time to trust the Lord and to do what we can. As we pray, the Lord is able to open doors….Lead on Oh King Eternal.

God continued to work among the Bahnar people as well. Year in and year out, John and Betty continued to pray for the Bahnar people. John had a sheet of yellow note paper with dozens of Bahnar names on it. He prayed over the names till the list became worn and tattered.

The majority of the Bahnar live on the central plateau of the country and many of them had become evangelical believers. Between that plateau and the coastal plain there is a lower, smaller plateau where over 30,000 Bahnar live. In that area only a very few believers lived in a handful of villages. In one of the three districts there were no believers at all.

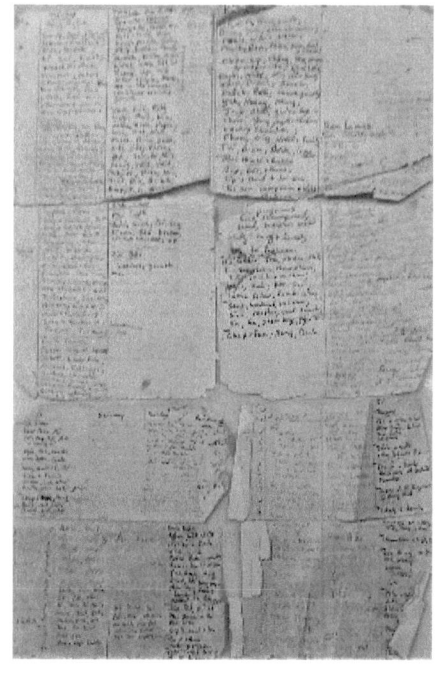

UNSTOPPABLE!

Smoking and drinking is the way of life for most Bahnar men from the time they are small boys. One man, Boot, who had been an orphan, decided he no longer wanted to smoke or drink like the rest of the people so he stopped.

Since the authorities knew that in other areas only the evangelical Christians didn't smoke or drink, they became suspicious that he had become a Christian. Since Christianity, especially evangelical Christianity, was thought of as the enemy, they began to give him a hard time. But he couldn't understand why.

When they accused him of being an evangelical Christian, Boot said, "I don't even know what you are talking about. I have never heard that term before."

But then he became interested in what they were saying and asked them where these Christians lived. They told him, "Up in the hills, at the top of the pass."

The Holy Spirit put such an earnest desire in Boot's heart for something better than his present way of life that he decided to go on foot to visit the area where the Christians lived.

It took him three days to reach the top of the pass. When he entered the first Bahnar village, Boot immediately met a fine Christian man who was the father-in-law of the local lay pastor. The seeker told the man that he wanted to find out about Christianity, and the father-in-law then led him to the Lord.

Boot then returned to his village and told others about his new-found faith. Some began to believe in the Lord Jesus.

UNSTOPPABLE!

Life suddenly got even more difficult. One person vowed to kill him. His plan, along with his friends, was to get drunk enough that he would be uninhibited and kill Boot. But in their drunkenness, he and his friends got into an argument. Now very angry and depressed, instead of killing Boot, he killed himself.

A second man also threatened to kill Boot. But before he could do it, he fell from a tree he was felling and broke his back. The Lord preserved Boot's life once again!

One time, Boot was captured, hung by his feet and beaten with the butt of a rifle. Undeterred, he continued to tell people about Jesus.

By the time John and Betty first heard this story, twelve people had believed in his village. Some lay evangelists from the other Bahnar area were making frequent trips to help support the fledgling church. It was with joy that John and Betty were able to help provide money to buy a bike for Boot. The Lord called him out of sin and darkness and used him to bring the Gospel to this totally unreached area.

One day a Bahnar man from Kontum was in his field. As he was working, he saw the ghost of a dead man. Terror gripped him. He knew about the Virgin Mary so he cried, "O Mary, please help me!" But the ghost remained.

He remembered Jesus' name so he cried, "O Jesus, please help me!"

Immediately the ghost disappeared. The man went to people he knew believed in Jesus and said he wanted to follow Jesus too.

UNSTOPPABLE!

After becoming a believer, he went back home to his village. One day a child was very sick and close to death. He prayed that the Lord would heal this child and the child was healed immediately. God also delivered him from his addiction to alcohol. He wanted to give up smoking as well so asked another Bahnar believer to pray for him.

He couldn't understand the Vietnamese Scriptures well but when he received the scriptures in his own language it was totally different. He could understand! He then went to share with others in his village about Jesus.

In 2008 Betty wrote:

> When we were in Southeast Asia last fall our translator friend gave us two "miracle books," you might call them. One was a revision of the New Testament we had been involved in years ago. This revision was published with full permission of the government! The second was a publication in memory of the gospel first coming to that highland area 65 years ago. In it were photographs of all the congregations, around 65 in all. Many of the congregations have hundreds of believers, and this was verified by these photographs.
>
> The scripture has been going out by radio in their language for over 30 years. In a certain area where there were only a few Christians or none at all, the people had enough money to buy radios of their own. They loved to listen to these programs, and so when they came into contact with believers, they began turning to Christ.
>
> We thought there were very few churches with small congregations, but even here there are several congregations with a total of almost 1,000 people, who have confessed Christ as Savior! Praise the Lord!

UNSTOPPABLE!

On April 18, 2008 the amazing news arrived that the official government permission for printing the revised New Testament in diglot (Bahnar and Vietnamese) had been granted. The following day John finished editing the Semantic Structure Analysis (SSA) commentary of Revelation and sent the manuscript off for publication. John had another deadline; getting the SSA commentary on Ephesians sent off to be included in the Translator's Workplace 5.0 translation software.

In August 2008, Betty wrote:

> Last week we received an email message with an attached photo. It was a photo of the dedication of the revised Bahnar New Testament. The dedication was celebrated on June 22, 2008. In the photo there are about forty Bahnar pastors, lay preachers and translators. Each person is holding a copy of the NT and more copies are on the table in front of them. This book has both the Bahnar and national language NT, side by side and is published with the full permission of the government of the country. So it is with much praise to the Lord that we send this message to you, and with much thankfulness.

> Regarding the commentary-type helps written in English for translators around the world, a translator recently wrote: "I want to thank you for the decades of work you have done to make such helps possible. They make an enormous difference for us on the field actually translating and trying to exegete the various books, both

UNSTOPPABLE!

N.T. and O.T. Now with even more new translation programs beginning, their use will be multiplied. I sure hope such work continues and even compounds because there will always be those who translate God's Word."

Persevering Even through the Twilight Years (2009-13)

These were exciting days because of all that God was doing, but not without struggles. John had been suffering severe pain in his stomach for quite some time. This eventually was diagnosed as being the H-pylori infection; thankfully not cancer.

Betty also had good reports from her MRI which showed for the second year in a row that the small growth in her brain had not changed. Also, the biopsy of a suspicious looking growth removed from her face was benign.

The living situation on every trip to South East Asia was not easy at their age, now in their 70s. John and Betty had been taking trips every year since official requests for their help had come in 1998. They ate, slept and worked in their 16-foot square room day after day.

The teams from different languages who came to work with them arrived before light and left after dark. After lunch they would all lie down and try to rest for a short while, all in the same room.

Betty and John never went outside; they only stared out the slats of the window shutters. The slats slanted downwards which meant that for weeks on end John and Betty could never see the sky, only what was passing by in the narrow alley. For exercise, they walked back and forth in their room for a half hour every night.

The translators from six languages John and Betty were consulting for also faced many difficulties and obstacles. Sometimes they were hindered by disease like dengue fever or TB, another time by a destructive typhoon. While one of the translators was checking scripture, he received news that his grandson had a fatal motorcycle accident.

Making sure the scriptures were communicating clearly and accurately was not always easy. Sometimes the answer to whether a verse was communicating clearly was, "The Bahnar will understand every word of these scriptures but will have no idea what they mean!" Despite these and other challenges Betty wrote home to their prayer partners saying:

> But what a special privilege to spend **all** day **every** day together with the translators looking at the Word of God trying to determine the meaning of each verse, and then encouraging the translators to express that meaning clearly in their languages. Extremely difficult. Extremely challenging. Humanly speaking it is an impossible job. What an awesome responsibility, but what a tremendous blessing and privilege God has entrusted to us, and TO

UNSTOPPABLE!

YOU, our partners. It would never happen without your part on your knees.

In 2009 John and Betty prayed about their next trip. The Lord gave them peace that they should only go for five weeks instead of the usual 11-12 weeks. Each trip was very important, but this one especially so because colleagues, who in the past had worked in two of the language groups whose translation John had been checking, were planning to join them for two weeks each. They were preparing to take on some of the responsibility for these two translation projects.

In 2010 John and Betty prepared to check 211 chapters of the Old and New Testament with translators from five language groups. Just before they left the U.S. Betty was sick with the flu. She spent four days in the hospital and barely recovered in time to pack for the trip. It was important that they go. One of the New Testaments they were checking was coming near to completion, and there were just five books left to translate for the Bahnar Old Testament.

It was exciting to see the church growing and reaching out in each of these five language groups, and to see them producing hymn books, recording the Jesus Film, and revising the New Testament with help from the Bankers. Working at least eight hours a day checking was getting harder and harder on their eyes as they were growing older.

Thankfully John and Betty had a good trip. John was able to finish the last couple books of the whole New Testament for one of the language groups and made significant progress checking NT books in three other languages. Despite a serious reaction for several days because of eating mushrooms, Betty was able to check Proverbs and over half of Jeremiah in Bahnar.

Right after their 2010 trip, Yohansi, the main translator for the Bahnar Old Testament had a very serious stroke. Although he had recovered some by the time the Bankers arrived for their 2011 trip, he still walked very slowly. He could write, but it was hard for anyone to read his writing. He often struggled to find a solution when there were problem passages in the translation. This made the translation work slow and especially difficult as they were working through one of the hardest books—Ezekiel.

In 2012, at 78, John suffered a stroke which affected his vision and left him with the inability to swallow properly. It was difficult for his eyes to focus when working on translation or editing SSA commentaries.

With a feeding tube, his strength gradually returned so that he could walk around slowly. With therapy he endeavored to strengthen the muscles in his throat so that he could swallow.

John soon began to struggle with recurring pneumonia. After five bouts he "graduated to glory" on May 2, 2013. There was much sorrow around the world at his passing. This humble but resilient warrior in the spiritual battle had helped so many people.

Freddy Boswell, the Executive Director of SIL, wrote the following for John's memorial service:

> I think today of John's excellent leadership of the Semantic and Structural Analysis team; his own work on the SSAs as general editor; his and Betty's untiring work over several decades to help deliver God's Word to the peoples of Southeast Asia through their translation and consulting work; and of his deep, passionate commitment for the Kingdom of God.
>
> My favorite memory of John Banker's story centers around a 'discovery' that was voiced at a meeting several years ago at the Translation Section of the International Forum of Bible Agencies. I was giving an SIL report on the development and progress of SIL translation helps, and I came to the point in my report about the Semantic and Structural Analysis series. Suddenly, Dr. Phil Towner, who was the Global Translation Director for the United Bible Societies, said to me in the presence of the group, "Isn't there an SSA on Titus?" I said "Yes, John Banker was the author of that volume." Dr Towner said, "Howard Marshall and I used that when we wrote the International Critical Commentary on the Pastoral Epistles. We really were helped by it!"

UNSTOPPABLE!

For those not aware of why what I just shared is significant, let me explain: 1) Phil Towner is a widely recognized and published Greek scholar and author, and currently the Dean of the Eugene A. Nida Institute for Biblical Scholarship of the American Bible Society; 2) I.H. Marshall is widely recognized as one of the world's leading New Testament scholars; 3) the International Critical Commentary has long been one of the premier scholarly resources for students and scholars of the Greek New Testament. *And these men were acknowledging the work of John Banker as an excellent contribution to their own scholarly endeavors!*

Not long after the meeting, I remember sharing with John what Dr. Towner had said to me. He responded simply without words, reflexively choosing what seemed to be almost a nervous, or embarrassed sort of soft giggle and smile...and then he just returned to his business at hand! That was John—deflective of praise, and appearing content to occupy a place of humble service in God's Kingdom.

I remember him as deep,
    steady,
        one we could count on,
            a man of insight and wisdom,
                and of a wealth of knowledge and
scholarship.

At John's death, Betty received other letters as well. From across the world came a letter from the Bahnar that when translated read, "He was a great man who helped us to translate the Bible....Tell his wife and his children that we love GRANDFATHER BANKER so much we cannot explain by our words how much we love him."

UNSTOPPABLE!

He Who Calls is Faithful (2013-15)

A few months later Betty wrote:

It is over three months now since GrandDadJack went to be with the Lord. I am very thankful for God's gracious help each day—some days are rather overwhelming but the Lord is teaching me to focus on His goodness and mercy to both of us. Working my way through the lengthy legal process, etc. best described by, "Hurry up so we can wait" is a challenge. It is a special blessing though to find that when I don't have a clue what to do, the Lord provides someone who does.

Three weeks ago our director came to talk about finishing the Bahnar Old Testament project....So I have been working almost full time on Ezekiel. You will recall that Ezekiel is the last book to be checked in order to finish the Bahnar OT. The good news is that I am now working on chapter 16—a very long complicated one. When I get through chapter 17, I will send the manuscript to the Bahnar translators by email. They will then look at the suggested revisions and make the appropriate changes in their manuscript. In the meantime, they have been going through their manuscript of Ezekiel chapters 18-48, which they translated some time ago, to check for exegetical accuracy and naturalness—does it really read like the people speak? They will then send it to me, also through a go-between, for me to check and then return to them.

I much prefer the "face-to-face" method of checking, but this is the best we can do right now. After already translating 38 OT books, they should be able to do it this way fairly easily. Please pray for the Lord's wisdom for them and for me. Working on Ezekiel has been good therapy, but I sure do miss GrandDadJack's help. He was always there to discuss difficult passages with me. Ezekiel has plenty of them!

Meanwhile, Betty's eyesight was significantly deteriorating due to macular degeneration, glaucoma, and cataracts. She spent hours sitting at the computer with her face just a few inches from the screen trying to read the drafts of the Bahnar Scriptures sent to her to check them for accuracy. Her large magnifying glass was her constant companion as she struggled to read the commentaries to better understand the Hebrew meaning of the text and make sure it had been applied to the translation. Cataract surgery was scheduled, but would be complicated because she also had astigmatism.

About this time, Tsedu, who John had trained many years previously, finished the translation of the Old Testament in his language. Ernie Lee had taken over from John the task of checking the scriptures in Tsedu's language. Tsedu and Ernie traveled to Tsedu's home area and found a thriving church, eager to have the whole Bible in their language. The celebration and dedication of the Bible was attended by three to four thousand people, with four choirs of around 100 people each, singing their praises to God.

Despite the loss of her dearly loved husband, her failing eyesight and aging body, God fulfilled His unstoppable purpose in Betty. Her cataract surgery enabled her to see well enough to finish the final checking process of the Bahnar Old Testament. By God's grace and with His help she finished at age 80. However, her health didn't allow her to take the long trip across the ocean to attend the dedication celebration. Her daughter, Kathy, agreed to go in her place.

Kathy had married the grandson of Grammy Payton, and the son of Pastor Hervey and Shirley Taber who had so faithfully prayed for the Bankers for many years. Kathy and her husband Mark went to the dedication of the Bahnar Bible in John and Betty's place. Official government permission arrived for them to attend just three days before the dedication took place. Since leaving the people they loved in the Bahnar villages in 1975, John and Betty had never been able to return to the central highlands where they lived.

Back in the U.S., Betty had a few surprise visitors. One of the visitors was the grandson of the district chief who first welcomed the Bankers to come work with the Bahnar, and whose brother Om was their first language helper and whose sister worked in their house many years previously.

Another visitor said, "Do you know Yon? I'm her great granddaughter." Yon had been the first one to teach Betty Bahnar during the two weeks they were living in the Bahnar communal house.

The Bahnar visitors summed up the purpose of their visit, "We have come to thank you and Grandfather [John] for what you did for our people by translating God's Word into our language so we could know the true living God." These were third and fourth generation Bahnar believers! And now the Bahnar Bible was even available in the "language" of the young generation—in YouVersion for everyone with a smart phone.

Betty's daughter, Kathy, and her husband Mark flew to Viet Nam for the dedication of the Bahnar Bible in December 2015. Kathy had many wonderful childhood memories of her home so long ago. One clear and dear image was of a tiny split bamboo church with only a handful of believers.

When Mark and Kathy arrived in the village for the Bible dedication, they found things very different. Instead of a small bamboo church there now stood a large beautiful church building facing a forest of rubber trees and purple mountains in the distance. Pine trees lined the sides of the road leading to the new church building which sat 1,000 people. People filled all the seats in the building, while others stood in the doorways, peered in through the open window, and overflowed the porchways like grain in a basket heaped up to the top, shaken down and spilling over. Many more from the surrounding areas wanted to attend but were not granted permission.

UNSTOPPABLE!

The Bahnar standing outside warmly welcomed Mark and Kathy and ushered them to the seats prepared for them near the front. As the Tabers walked down the long aisle, people were joyfully singing in their language.

Mark and Kathy looked out on a sea of faces turned toward them, singing praise to God and worshipping Him.

That moment was like being in heaven and listening to the heavenly host of saints singing the Song of the Lamb. Amazingly, Betty was able to watch that scene on her computer via video Skype from Mark's cell phone for a few minutes before the signal was lost.

At the time of the dedication Bahnar believers numbered over 26,000 and still growing today. Tears flowed from Kathy's eyes as she thought of her father, who was now in heaven, and her mother, both of whom had never returned to see the fruit of their labor. She thought about her parents' great sacrifice and perseverance, and their faith in God: a faith that obeys even when unable to see the road ahead; a faith based on God's promises, some of which He will accomplish for us and those we love only after we pass on to glory.

Kathy was overwhelmed by God's great faithfulness and unfailing love, not only to her family, but to the dearly loved Bahnar people.

Kathy and Mark were led to the front and seated with the Bahnar and Vietnamese pastors, some who traveled a great distance to be present. The service was three hours long. Four large choirs sang, each from a different age group. Two of the three choirs had 200-300 people each. The history of how the Bible came to the Bahnar was told. A sermon was preached in Bahnar and interpreted into Vietnamese.

After the service, people approached Kathy and asked if she knew who they were. Amazingly, she was able to recognize them even though she hadn't seen them for 40 years and was not quite a teenager when she left. They asked about her mother, and with tears told of their grief because of her father's death.

UNSTOPPABLE!

After the service there was a celebration feast. Then Kathy and Mark were taken to the home of the main Old Testament translator who had also recently died. His family showed them the upper room where he had worked for many hours translating the Bible, as well as the bigger room where the translation committee had worked as a team and the church had met for many years. They told many stories of faith, hard work, sacrifice, suffering and perseverance with great emotion and joy for all that God had done.

This is a story about courage. It is a story of partnership. It is about the Bahnar and the other peoples of Viet Nam and those who love them. It includes people from various missions and outreaches, the national church, the Bible Society, God's people from various walks of life and over fifty years of prayer by many people around the world. What an incredible story of faith and the perseverance of God's people.

But in reality, at the very heart of it all, this is a story about God and His incredible faithfulness.

His love is unstoppable!

UNSTOPPABLE!

Epilogue

After my father passed away in 2013, I began to think about writing a book about his life. It took a few years before I started. Then between my other responsibilities it took several years to organize and read all my parents' letters, pull them together into a book, and fill in the background information from other sources.

This book started as a tribute to my father but in the process, I couldn't miss the huge impact my mother also had, as they were both an inseparable part of God's unstoppable plan. Being confined during COVID-19 for the past eight months, my mother and I spent many hours talking. She filled me in on the many details of her life, which I added to this book.

About the time I finished writing, my mother suddenly became very ill and was diagnosed with pancreatic cancer. The day the oncologist told her the news, she replied, "I am not expecting to live forever. Well, actually I am expecting to live forever in heaven, and do you know how I know that I will?"

A glorious smile suddenly radiated from mom's face and she was full of joy. She looked absolutely beautiful!

She continued, "The Bible tells us. It tells us how sin came into the world and how we all became sinners but God sent His Son to die on the cross for us so that He could take away our sins and make us right with God and so that we could live forever in heaven with Him. My husband will be there, too, and many people. In my house I have the Bible in the Bahnar language of Vietnam which we translated. Because of that Bible there are going to be many of those people there too."

She took a breath and said, "I am not afraid to die. I am not afraid to die at all!"

Mom went downhill very fast. But every time someone came to visit her, they too were blessed because her love and faith in God shone brightly from her. She kissed the young African American hospice aide saying, "I love you. I love you, I love you." She told others who shared their struggles with her that now was the time to really have faith in God.

She basked in the pleasure of having four generations of family around to celebrate her 86th birthday. One day she said, "I am going up there [to heaven] but I am sure having a great time down here." She said this as she laid in bed hardly able to move while the cancer was taking over her body.

A few days later on October 18, 2020 she peacefully passed into the presence of Jesus while scripture was being read to her. In the background the old hymn, "I Love to Tell the Story," was playing as she took her last breath. Yes—*that* Story of Jesus and His unstoppable love—for Dad and Mom, the Bahnar people, and for all who believe.

UNSTOPPABLE!

Sources

By Life or By Death. James C. Hefley, Zondervan Publishing House, Grand Rapids, MI, 1969.

Captured! Carolyn Paine Miller, Christian Herald Books, Chapaqua, NY, 1977.

No Time for Tombstones: Life And Death in the Vietnamese Jungle. James and Marti Hefley, Tyndale House Publishers Inc., Wheaton, IL, 1974.

Sadie Busse Sieker 1903-1987 Exceeding Abundantly Above. Sadie Sieker, Karen Lynip, Editor, Privately Published, 1986.

The Joy of a Loving Jonathan. Hugh Steven, Private publication, 1974. Added epilogue in 2003 in Chiang Mai, Thailand.